Praise for Dante Lee

*"**Dante Lee** didn't wait for an opportunity to be presented . . . he created one himself and made history in the process."*

— **Margena A. Christian**, Editor, *Ebony*

*"**Dante Lee** is a perfect example of someone who has translated perseverance and determination into success. He has worked tremendously hard to create a business with multiple revenue streams to reach critical niche markets in this country."*

— **Neil Foote**, Director, Media Relations, Tom Joyner Foundation

*"**Dante** possesses an entrepreneurial spirit that only a few can aspire to reach. His self-directed energy has inspired me and countless others who have come in contact with him as we seek to connect with the world. I'm honored to endorse him and his work. . ."*

— **Edward Foxworth III**, Owner, Foxworth Marketing Group

*"**Dante** does not just speak . . . he walks his talks! His insights . . . will help you maximize any business opportunity."*

— **Andrew Morrison**, founder and president of The Small Business Camp

*"**Dante** is a brilliant young CEO that I would highly recommend in business and personally. His efforts in building BlackNews.com and BlackPR.com have been quite admirable . . . I expect **Dante** to continue to raise the bar when it comes to running a business and serving the needs of the multicultural market. Did I mention BlackHistory.com!?"*

— **William Moss**, president & CEO, LeeMoss Media

Black
Business
SECRETS

Black Business SECRETS

500 Tips, Strategies, and Resources
for the African American Entrepreneur

Dante Lee

SMILEYBOOKS

DISTRIBUTED BY HAY HOUSE, INC.
Carlsbad, California • New York City
London • Sydney • Johannesburg
Vancouver • Hong Kong • New Delhi

Library of Congress Control Number: 2010933583

Tradecover ISBN: 978-1-4019- 2954-1
Digital ISBN: 978-1-4019-2955-8

14 13 12 11   5 4 3 2
1st edition, November 2010
2nd edition, January 2011

Printed in the United States of America

Black Business Secrets is dedicated to transforming the devastating statistics that African Americans are much more likely to fail in business than their white, Asian, or Hispanic counterparts due to lack of fundamental business education, insufficient economic development, and resources.

Any entrepreneur of any race can benefit from this book, but this content has been specifically designed to challenge and inspire African Americans because our need is greater and our potential is now limitless.

CONTENTS

FOREWORD

ENTREPRENEURSHIP IS IN OUR DNA

by Randal Pinkett, CEO of BCT Partners
and Winner of NBC's *The Apprentice*

African Americans have always been successful in entrepreneurship—whether or not we've profited from it, and whether or not we've realized it.

Think about it. Entrepreneurship is about combining your passion and talents to create value in the world. African Americans have been doing this for centuries in business, government, nonprofits, schools, churches, and communities across the globe.

There are countless examples, from Garrett Morgan who invented the traffic signal, to George Washington Carver who invented peanut butter, to Nathaniel Alexander who invented the folding chair. And, of course, there's Madame "C.J." Walker who developed and marketed the most successful line of beauty and hair care products of her time. She went on to become the first female millionaire of any color.

More recently, there's Bob Johnson, the mastermind behind BET; Cathy Hughes, who created Radio One and TV One; Oprah Winfrey, founder of Harpo Productions; Lisa Price, founder of Carol's Daughter; David Steward, chairman of World Wide Technology; Magic Johnson, who started Magic Johnson Enterprises; and the list goes on. All of their companies, by the way, are multimillion or multibillion-dollar enterprises.

Furthermore, there are hundreds of thousands of barbershops, hair/nail salons, doctors' offices, law firms, consulting firms, advertising agencies, publishing companies, auto dealerships, cleaning companies, etc., owned and operated by African Americans.

Because our ancestors were successful in business, it is justifiable to say that it's in *our* DNA to also be successful in business.

African Americans have long demonstrated that we are fully capable of creating our own success like anyone else. As a result, nowadays, more blacks than ever before can call themselves successful and profitable business owners.

Despite this fact, the numbers are still very disturbing. Recent data from the Census Bureau suggests that African American business owners are still more likely to fail than their white counterparts. How can this be, if entrepreneurship is in our DNA?

I would argue that DNA—the genetic code we are born with—can be *figuratively* altered over time by our behavior. Consider that a person's hair color is also in the DNA—but using dyes and chemicals, hair can easily be changed to any color. Even the shape of a person's nose can be altered through plastic surgery.

Likewise, many African Americans have consciously or unconsciously altered their DNA through a sometimes simple, and at other times complex, cocktail of inner and outer influences. Instead of capitalizing on their "genetic code" of confidence, assertiveness, and determination to become successful entrepreneurs, some allow factors such as racism, discrimination, and other forms of unfair treatment to interfere with their natural business acumen and weigh them down mentally and emotionally. As a result, they give up and settle for less. However, it's been proven time and again that even in the face of racism and discrimination, anyone, including African Americans, can be successful in business.

Some alter their DNA by opting to follow the "traditional" path of working for someone else, being unwilling to take a leap of faith to launch a new venture. Others simply never envision themselves owning a business despite their "genetic code" for incredible business ability. This was once the case for me. Fortunately, it was in learning the example of other African American business owners that I aspired to become an entrepreneur. Thanks to them, I overcame my challenges so that today I proudly serve as the co-founder, chairman, and CEO of BCT Partners, a multimillion-dollar management consulting and information technology services firm. In other words, entrepreneurship IS in our DNA, and as speaker and author George Fraser says, "Success runs in our race."

My friend and colleague, Dante Lee, has written a wonderful book for you to truly overcome your challenges, become successful in business, and embrace the entrepreneurial DNA that lies within you. This book is for aspiring entrepreneurs who are looking to get started, and for existing entrepreneurs who are looking for guidance and insight regarding the next steps to take.

I invite you to read every page carefully, give major consideration to each point, and to immediately activate and energize the entrepreneurship DNA inherited from our ancestors!

Randal Pinkett

WHAT IT MEANS TO BE A BLACK ENTREPRENEUR

Being an entrepreneur in America isn't easy. It's a delicate and complex balancing act that can lead to success or failure. Most businesses don't last more than two years. Most that fail suffer from inadequate resources, funding, and/or business acumen. However, in recent years increasing numbers of people have attempted to go into business for themselves. Despite a lagging economy and a recession that resembles a depression, young entrepreneurs are on the rise. Much of this is due to fewer job prospects for graduating students throughout the country. Thus many turn to business ownership in the hope of building a future for themselves in an unstable and unsure economy.

Becoming an entrepreneur is difficult enough in these trying times, but becoming a black entrepreneur comes with added stress and challenges not faced by the average business owner. While many in our society tout the notion of a new age of awareness and a new level of racial equality, those who are biased haven't caught up. Maybe they didn't get the memo. While it's a novel idea that racial inequality has all but vanished, it is not yet a reality. Black entrepreneurs continue to face some of the same challenges they faced fifty or more years ago, such as dealing with a double standard when applying for financing.

This is not to say that opportunities haven't been made available to give small black businesses a chance. But the fact remains that it sometimes takes black business owners longer than others

1

to achieve the same results. Yet, despite large and frequent obstacles, many black businesses have thrived, sometimes surpassing mainstream white-owned businesses in quality of products and services. Take Carol's Daughter for example. A business that started in a kitchen now has reached multi-million dollar status. Women of color who use Carol's Daughter products revel in beauty products that reflect their culture and lifestyle. But there's still a gap to be closed and much work to be done to put black businesses on par with mainstream white businesses.

Selling our goods and services to other countries hasn't made this journey any easier. While the nation as a whole suffers from the loss of jobs, blacks bear the brunt of the lagging economy. This disparity is evidenced in the higher percentage of blacks who are unemployed, and the disproportionate wage difference between blacks and whites. When firms go south and to the East, it's not only the jobs that leave but also the resources used to make the products. A black business owner who, let's say, would like to get into the furniture-making business no longer has easy access to the types of wood needed for the venture. America supplies less and less lumber while more and more is imported from other countries. A usual excuse is that cheaper labor elsewhere allows profit to be made.

Such use of outside resources that we could easily provide domestically makes it difficult for black business owners to enter such a niche market. Connection to those overseas sellers becomes a closed market not easily accessible (if at all) to blacks wishing to join the ranks of furniture makers.

While farmers are being paid not to grow certain commodities that were once staple American products, the economy continues to suffer from the export of jobs and services, and the import of goods that were once made in America. This dismantling of American labor and resources leaves black entrepreneurs fewer choices as to which economic area to participate in effectively.

Such a plethora of challenges gives satisfaction to black business owners who have reached some level of success and adds deep meaning to their ventures. From this struggle comes a strong desire to provide high quality service to consumers. Climbing toward success on a much steeper mountain has made the fruits of labor sweeter for black entrepreneurs around the country.

HISTORIC STRUGGLES OF BLACKS IN BUSINESS

Blacks have been confronted with numerous difficulties throughout our history in the Americas. In Oklahoma in the early 1900s, Greenwood, Oklahoma—also known as Black Wall Street—was founded in North Tulsa because of those struggles and thrived. The success of the town was due to its inhabitants' determination to build financial independence at a time when blacks were generally prevented from participating in the economic prosperity of America. Blacks of the era couldn't shop in certain neighborhoods, banks refused business and private loans, and living comfortably was by and large reserved for white America. But for the most part, the 10,000 citizens of Black Wall Street found everything a person of color needed to have a normal life and a successful financial future.

Little Africa, as it was also known, was sometimes described as a mini-Beverly Hills. It was considered the golden door of the black community. The infrastructure was top notch. A dollar circulated 100 times before leaving the community—a feat unheard of in black America today, where a dollar leaves the community within minutes.

Greenwood counted doctors, lawyers, realtors and PhDs among its residents. One was a Dr. Berry who owned the bus system. His income then was $500 per day. Nothing to be sneezed at in 1910—or today. There were 15 physicians, two newspapers, more than a dozen churches (more per capita than in the white community), 21 restaurants and two movie theaters, as well as pawnshops, brothels, and jewelry stores. Greenwood was a complete society.

During those years, Oklahoma had only two airports, so it was a huge feat for six blacks to actually own their own planes. Little

Africa boasted about 600 businesses within 36 square blocks. Education was a top priority and every child was afforded a quality education. The town glittered with racial pride that manifested itself in the clear strength of its economy. It's even rumored that some whites who were refused a bank loan in their own community attempted to get loans in Black Wall Street.

As many already know, Black Wall Street was not to last. Today, the attack on Little Africa is known as the Tulsa Race Riot of 1921. In less than 12 hours the town became a wasteland. Nothing but rubble remained. Greenwood was torched by local whites and Ku Klux Klan members. The fires smoldered for days, destroying what was once a beacon of hope for blacks in America.

Black Wall Street became the symbol of a dream deferred. Whites were not going to have a successful black town on their watch. This was confirmed when many witnessed whites standing on the outskirts of their town, circling it, watching—like spectators at a lynching. The human suffering was gruesome: some 3,000 African Americans—men, women and children—were murdered and about 600 successful businesses were lost.

Despite the tragic end to Black Wall Street, it remains a testament to our innate ability to achieve success whatever the obstacles set before us. Blacks have always had the intellectual capital and physical ability to create thriving communities on our own terms.

One account is *Black Wall Street: A Lost Dream* and its companion documentary, *Black Wall Street: A Black Holocaust in America* by Jay Wilson and Ron Wallace. From area historians and elderly survivors, these authors chronicled the events of June 1921. A more thorough account is "The Tulsa Race Riot" by Scott Ellsworth, (http://www.tulsareparations.org/TulsaRiot.htm).

The Tulsa Riot represents one in a long list of outrages against African Americans in the United States. Black businesses and communities are continually sabotaged in various ways, often by subterfuge, sometimes by refusals that make no sense. "You are over-qualified." "You need more collateral for this loan." "Your income is not sufficient." There's often some predictable rationale behind the refusal to either hire or provide a small business loan.

In the same period there was another flourishing community in rural Levy County, Florida called Rosewood. In the first week of January 1923, a violent conflict completely decimated Rosewood, a primarily black, self-sufficient town. Settled in 1845, its name came from the reddish color of cut cedar wood. Initially, the population was both white and black, but by 1900 had become primarily African American. Two powerful black families were the pillars of the community, building it into an economic success during a time when blacks were still disenfranchised from voting through trickery or by rules that made the ballot box inaccessible. Allegations that a black man raped a white woman led to the destruction of Rosewood—in a way reminiscent of Black Wall Street. Just two years after the burning of Little Africa, Rosewood was destroyed. It begs the question: Was this a coordinated effort to dismantle any black community that was economically self-sufficient? Despite such dramatic setbacks, there's always been a strong sense of determination amongst African Americans to gain economic independence.

Some may wonder how it is that individuals who look like us find some level of success. Small doses of black success do not disturb the comfort of whites. But collectively the African American community's attempts at business success and economic independence tend to meet with great resistance. One individual who *was* allowed to thrive was Madam C.J. Walker.

Born Sarah Breedlove on December 23, 1867, this daughter of former slaves transformed herself from an uneducated laundress and farm laborer on a Delta, Louisiana (population 239 in the 2000 census) plantation into one of the most successful self-made female entrepreneurs. Orphaned at age seven, Walker survived with her sister, Louvenia, by working in cotton fields. Her sole heir, Lelia (later named A'Lelia Walker), was born on June 6, 1885. Her start in business was prompted by a scalp ailment she contracted during the 1890s. She tried almost everything, but the condition persisted until she used a treatment that she created. It was not long after marrying her third husband, Charles

Joseph Walker, that she founded her own business and began selling Madam Walker's Wonderful Hair Grower, a scalp conditioning and healing formula. Walker claimed at the time that the formula was revealed to her in a dream.

As a new entrepreneur, Madame Walker understood what it took to build a business. For the first year and a half, she traveled throughout the black South, selling her products door to door. She gave demonstrations in churches and lodges, devising ever more effective sales and marketing strategies. She immersed herself in the business and learned from experience. By 1908, she'd temporarily settled in Pittsburgh and opened Lelia College to train Walker "hair culturists."

In early 1910, Madame Walker settled in Indianapolis. There she built a factory, a hair and manicure salon, and another training school. Within a year her name went viral, and black newspapers took notice when she gave $1,000 to the colored YMCA for its building fund.

Madame Walker lived a lush life, enjoying her wealth to the fullest. Her success demonstrates that blacks can attain a piece of the American dream through a keen focus on what it takes to be a business owner. Madam Walker concentrated on product quality, business integrity, and marketing. With the right product, all you need to do is find the consumers—reach the people who need what you have to offer—and make sure your infrastructure can manage the demand once you reach your audience. You may have a great product and effective marketing, but if the final step—delivery—isn't mastered, all the previous hard work could be for naught. Ensure you're able to deliver.

DANTE LEE—MY STORY

I am a marketing guru, a PR maven, and an award-winning business coach. *I deliver on my promises.* As president and CEO of Diversity City Media and cofounder of Lee Moss Media, both based in Columbus, Ohio, I've earned my keep. Through hard work, determination, and business acumen, I've built my businesses to a level where they have become more than a mere need for black entrepreneurs, but a necessity for marketing products and information to the black community. My award-winning companies have helped clients reach African American consumers through online advertising and public relations. As owners of the largest network of premium African American web properties (including Black-PR.com, BlackNews.com, HBCUConnect.com, BlackHistory.com, BlackWomenConnect.com, BlackExperts.com, etc.), my partner, William Moss, and I are highly regarded in the internet marketing industry. Over a ten-year span, our companies have consistently generated millions of dollars in revenue.

Our long-time clients include Nationwide Insurance, Ford Motors, Toyota, McDonald's, BET, NASCAR, Verizon, and TV One.

I've been recognized by MSNBC, CNN, and scores of newspapers and magazines. *Ebony* magazine named me one of the "Top 30 Young Leaders for 2006" and profiled me as a successful black business owner in 2010. I was nominated by *Black Enterprise* magazine for the 2006 Small Business of the Year Award, and was highlighted in three back-to-back issues. I currently serve as a motivational speaker and diversity consultant, and have addressed groups ranging from the African American Business Summit (AABS), the Tavis Smiley Leadership Institute, the National Association of Black Telecommunications Professionals (NABTP), and the Booker T. Washington Economic Development Summit.

Born and raised in the Washington, DC area, I graduated from Bowie State University with a bachelor's degree in computer science, completing my four-year program in three years.

I share who I am with you to give you a frame of reference as you consider how the business information I provide on business can assist you. Take all of it, take some of it, or take a single concept—my hope is that by learning from my in-the-trenches experiences your business will reward you with the success and satisfaction that I have been allowed to claim.

WHY I WANT TO COACH YOU

As an entrepreneur who has met with success, I believe I'm more than qualified to assist you in reaching your goal of becoming a successful business owner or, if you're already a business owner, to help you build your business further.

As I've mentioned, running a business is difficult and complex but isn't nuclear physics. There are numerous ways in which entrepreneurs can start, build, and maintain an enterprise. While there's no one-size-fits-all method, what I can share with you are some tools that most business owners use to help boost their sales. Look at this book as the black business bible. Read it, digest it, and use it. And always remember to share it.

Black Business Secrets is more than a simple how-to. It's a coaching plan that initiates you into the entrepreneurial mindset and a compendium of resources that can lead you down the road to success. Don't merely follow each suggestion blindly; instead use what's presented here in a way that allows you to create your own path toward success. Add to what's offered here and, more importantly, share what you've added to these offerings with others. Expand the boundaries of knowledge so that the next generation won't have to reinvent the wheel.

Take from the wisdom of visionaries such as Bob Johnson, founder of BET, Tom Burrell, founder of Burrell Communications, Lisa Price, founder of Carol's Daughter, and Nadine Thompson, founder of Warm Spirit. These are just a few of the voices who'll guide you by sharing their stories—what they did, what they didn't do, and the mistakes they made that taught them valuable lessons.

This work breaks down the reasoning as to why now, more than ever, it makes good economic good sense to own your own business and how ownership can create financial independence. There is great satisfaction in knowing that you created something worth passing on to your children and other family members rather than slaving away at a 9 to 5 to create a strong and prosperous empire for some stranger that may last for generations, with no benefit to you. Your business is your empire, to be built from the ground up and to be passed from hand to hand within your family.

Knowing what's going on in the world of business gives you a leg up. Learn more about what's going on in federal, state, and local governments, Understand the intricacies and some of the pros and cons of outsourcing. Learn how the digital age could affect your business. Knowing your own mind is even more important. Always remember to be clear why you want to become an entrepreneur. While owning your own business can be rewarding and satisfying, it's hard work and not for the faint of heart. It is mentally challenging and sometimes physically strenuous, depending on the business you've chosen. Are you ready? What are the skills you must bring to the table? Have you effectively dissected your idea and done the research required to ensure your business idea is a viable one? Do you know your market? And do you have the resources to provide the goods or services you've promised?

A fundamental aspect of business is networking. While some might be shy to get their network on, it's critical that budding entrepreneurs peddle their goods and services to as many people as possible. This can only happen through marketing and advertising. While these take many forms, from door-to-door sales, to internet newsletters via e-mail, to smart phone advertisements, the concept and action required are the same. As a business owner you must address your market, meet your consumers, or become allied with your clients. Business transactions are very personal to both parties. It's important that you make yourself known not only to those you're trying to reach, and that you're transparent. Everything in a business relationship must be ethical and genuine.

Get to know your audience and don't be afraid to put yourself out front so your efforts are visible. Learn from some of the pros how networking can help you build a viable business that will last for a few lifetimes. Imagine building a business that can someday tout being 100 years old? Network, network, network. Someday that could turn into a history that you've made.

Black Business Secrets offers business tips that will help you get the ball rolling—from consulting to franchises to preparing to enter emerging markets. The book also sheds light on some unsound business decisions and how entrepreneurs can work themselves out of a rut they may find themselves in.

Contributions from experienced businesspeople have been central to compiling this wealth of information. They generously gave of their time to provide this warehouse of knowledge for business owners, aspiring and seasoned, young and old. Grab a cup of coffee or tea, kick off your shoes, take out your highlighter, and let this book give you the tools to ensure that your business will shine throughout the 21st century.

CHAPTER 2

BLACK BUSINESS THE REAL STORY

What is the real story? How many black businesses are out there? How are they doing? Bare facts can often tell an interesting story but they can't be taken merely at face value. We need to dissect the numbers to understand what we're looking at.

While black business as a whole still lags behind the mainstream, the success of the black business culture cannot be overstated. Rather than spend more time belaboring the injustices and obstacles that black business owners have had to transcend, let's instead shed light on the strides we've made. The July 10, 2010 report on 2007 business ownership data will help us do just that.

The latest Census Bureau data, *Preliminary Estimates of Business Ownership by Gender, Ethnicity, Race and Veteran Status: 2007*, from the U.S. Census Bureau's 2007 Survey of Business Owners and Self-Employed Persons (SBO), provides the only comprehensive, regularly collected source of information on minority business owners.

This preliminary report is the first of 10 reports on the characteristics of minority, women, and veteran-owned businesses and their owners scheduled for release over the next year.

SBO report highlights included:

The number of minority-owned businesses increased by 45.6 percent to 5.8 million between 2002 and 2007, more than twice the national rate of all U.S. businesses. In addition, the number of women-owned businesses increased 20.1 percent during the same period. The total number of U.S. businesses increased between 2002 and 2007 by 18.0 percent to 27.1 million.

Increases in the number of minority-owned businesses ranged from 60.5 percent for black-owned businesses to 17.9 percent for American Indian- and Alaska Native-owned businesses. Hispanic-owned businesses increased by 43.6 percent.

Receipts of minority-owned businesses rose 55.6 percent to $1.0 trillion between 2002 and 2007. Increases ranged from a high of 62.9 percent for Native Hawaiian- and Other Pacific Islander-owned businesses to 28.3 percent for American Indian- and Alaska Native-owned businesses. Over the same period, receipts of His-panic-owned and women-owned businesses increased by 55.5 per-cent and 27.0 percent respectively. Receipts of all U.S. businesses increased by 33.5 percent to $30.2 trillion.

ALL U.S. BUSINESSES

- Employer firms: Of the nation's 27.1 million businesses in 2007, roughly 5.8 million had paid employees. These businesses employed 118.7 million people, a 7.1 percent increase from 2002. Their payrolls totaled $4.9 trillion, up 28.2 percent from 2002, and their receipts totaled $29.2 trillion, up 33.8 percent.

- Nonemployer firms: An estimated 21.4 million businesses had no paid employees in 2007. Receipts at these firms totaled $972.7 billion, up 26.8 percent from 2002.

MINORITY-OWNED BUSINESSES

- Of the nation's 5.8 million minority-owned businesses in 2007, an estimated 5.0 million had no paid employees. Receipts of these nonemployer businesses totaled $164.4 billion.

- Among all minority-owned businesses, 768,147 had paid employees in 2007. These businesses employed 5.9 million people with a total payroll of $168.2 billion. Receipts for minority-owned businesses with employees totaled $864.2 billion.

- In 2007, 30.0 percent of minority-owned businesses were in repair and maintenance, personal and laundry services, and health care and social assistance.

- Minority-owned businesses accounted for 56.9 percent of businesses in Hawaii, which led the nation, followed by the District of Columbia, where 40.2 percent of businesses were minority-owned, and California, where 35.6 percent of businesses were minority-owned.

WOMEN-OWNED BUSINESSES

- The number of women-owned businesses totaled 7.8 million in 2007, up 20.1 percent from 2002. By comparison, men-owned businesses totaled 13.9 million, up 5.5 percent from 2002.

- In 2007, 31.9 percent of women-owned businesses were in repair and maintenance, personal and laundry services, and health care and social assistance.

WHITE-OWNED BUSINESSES

- The number of white-owned businesses increased by 13.6 percent to 22.6 million between 2002 and 2007. Receipts of these businesses totaled $10.3 trillion, up 24.1 percent from 2002.

- In 2007, 28.5 percent of white-owned businesses were in professional, scientific and technical services and construction.

BLACK-OWNED BUSINESSES

- There were 1.9 million black-owned businesses in 2007, up 60.5 percent from 2002. Receipts of these businesses totaled $137.4 billion, up 55.1 percent from 2002.

- In 2007, 37.6 percent of black-owned businesses were in health care and social assistance, repair and maintenance, and personal and laundry services.

- Black-owned businesses accounted for 28.2 percent of businesses in the District of Columbia, which led the nation, followed by Georgia, where 20.4 percent of businesses were black-owned, and Maryland, where 19.3 percent of businesses were black-owned.

ASIAN-OWNED BUSINESSES

- There were 1.6 million Asian-owned businesses in 2007, up 40.7 percent from 2002. Receipts of these businesses totaled $513.9 billion, up 57.3 percent from 2002.

- In 2007, 32.3 percent of Asian-owned businesses were in repair and maintenance; personal and laundry services; and professional, scientific and technical services.

- Asian-owned businesses accounted for 47.2 percent of businesses in Hawaii, 14.9 percent in California and 10.1 percent in New York.

NATIVE HAWAIIAN- AND OTHER PACIFIC ISLANDER-OWNED BUSINESSES

- The number of Native Hawaiian- and Other Pacific Islander-owned businesses totaled 38,881 in 2007, up 34.3 percent from 2002; receipts of these businesses totaled $7.0 billion, up 62.9 percent from 2002.

- Repair and maintenance, personal and laundry services, and construction accounted for 26.9 percent of all Native Hawaiian- and Other Pacific Islander-owned businesses.

- Native Hawaiian- and Other Pacific Islander-owned businesses accounted for 9.4 percent of businesses in Hawaii, highest among all states.

AMERICAN INDIAN- AND ALASKA NATIVE-OWNED BUSINESSES

- The number of American Indian- and Alaska Native-owned businesses totaled 237,386 in 2007, up 17.9 percent from 2002; total receipts of these businesses were $34.5 billion, up 28.3 percent from 2002.

- In 2007, 30.5 percent of American Indian- and Alaska Native-owned businesses were in construction, repair and maintenance, and personal and laundry services.

- American Indian- and Alaska Native-owned businesses accounted for 10.0 percent of businesses in Alaska, 6.3 percent in Oklahoma and 5.3 percent in New Mexico.

HISPANIC-OWNED BUSINESSES

- The number of Hispanic-owned businesses totaled 2.3 million in 2007, up 43.6 percent from 2002. Receipts of these businesses totaled $345.2 billion, up 55.5 percent from 2002.

- In 2007, 30.0 percent of Hispanic-owned businesses were in construction, repair and maintenance, and personal and laundry services.

- Hispanic-owned businesses accounted for 23.6 percent of businesses in New Mexico, 22.4 percent of businesses in Florida and 20.7 percent of businesses in Texas.

SUMMARY OF FINDINGS SURVEY OF BUSINESS OWNERS— BLACK-OWNED FIRMS 2007

The 2007 Survey of Business Owners (SBO) defines Black-owned businesses as firms in which Blacks own 51 percent or more of the stock or equity of the business. The 2007 SBO data were collected as part of the 2007 Economic Census from a sample of more than 2.3 million nonfarm businesses filing 2007 tax forms as individual proprietorships, partnerships, or any type of corporation, and with receipts of $1,000 or more.

In 2007, blacks owned 1.9 million nonfarm U.S. businesses, an increase of 60.5 percent from 2002. In 2007, Black-owned firms accounted for 7.1 percent of all nonfarm businesses in the United States, 0.8 percent of total employment and 0.5 percent of total receipts.

KIND OF BUSINESS CHARACTERISTICS

In 2007, 37.6 percent of Black-owned firms operated in the health care and social assistance industries, and the repair, maintenance, personal, and laundry services industries. Chart A shows the distribution of firms according to sector. Black-owned firms accounted for 13.2 percent of all U.S. businesses in these industries. Retail trade and health care and social assistance accounted for 27.5 percent of Black-owned business revenue.

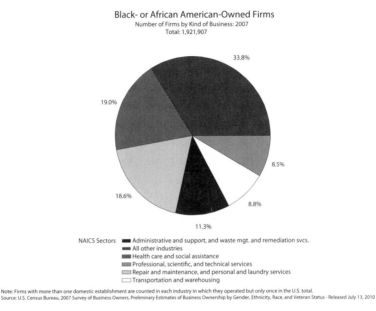

Black- or African American-Owned Firms
Number of Firms by Kind of Business: 2007
Total: 1,921,907

NAICS Sectors
- Administrative and support, and waste mgt. and remediation svcs.
- All other industries
- Health care and social assistance
- Professional, scientific, and technical services
- Repair and maintenance, and personal and laundry services
- Transportation and warehousing

Note: Firms with more than one domestic establishment are counted in each industry in which they operated but only once in the U.S. total.
Source: U.S. Census Bureau, 2007 Survey of Business Owners, Preliminary Estimates of Business Ownership by Gender, Ethnicity, Race, and Veteran Status - Released July 13, 2010

GEOGRAPHIC CHARACTERISTICS

New York had the most Black-owned firms at 204,093 (10.6 percent of all such firms), with receipts of $12.9 billion (9.4 percent of all Black-owned firm receipts). Georgia accounted for 183,876 Black-owned firms or 9.6 percent, with receipts of $8.9 billion or 6.5 percent, while Florida accounted for 181,469 Black-owned firms or 9.4 percent, with receipts of $10.7 billion or 7.8 percent. Texas was fourth with 154,255 Black-owned firms or 8.0 percent of all Black-owned firms, and 6.8 percent of receipts. While California was fifth in terms of numbers with 7.2 percent of all Black-owned firms, it was first in terms of revenue with receipts of $18.9 billion or 13.7 percent.

BLACK-OWNED EMPLOYER AND NONEMPLOYER FIRMS

In 2007, there were 106,779 Black-owned employer firms. These firms employed 920,198 persons with a total payroll of $23.9 billion, an increase of 22.0 percent and 36.2 percent respectively from 2002. In 2007, these firms generated $98.8 billion in receipts, an increase of 50.2 percent. Employer firms accounted for 5.6 percent of the total number of Black-owned firms and 71.9 percent of Black-owned firms' gross receipts. The average receipts for these employer firms was $925,651.

In 2007, there were 1.8 million Black-owned firms without paid employees. These firms generated $38.6 billion in receipts, an increase of 69.0 percent from 2002. In 2007, nonemployers accounted for 94.4 percent of the total number of Black-owned firms and 28.1 percent of gross receipts. The average receipts for these nonemployer firms was $21,270.

WHAT DOES IT ALL MEAN?

What does this all mean? How can we analyze these statistics to arrive at conclusions that serve the African American business community? Reading the statistics, you'll see that while blacks have made great strides in business, there is still a huge chasm between our achievements and the mainstream business community. While there were 1.9 million African American-owned businesses in the United States in 2007, that is not an appropriate percentage of the 27.1 million businesses that exist in the United States. Blacks own only 7.1 percent of U.S. companies but make up 12.8 percent of the U.S. population.

Of course, there was a time when blacks were not allowed to own businesses at all. It is an incredible achievement that we have made such a huge dent in that socioeconomic barrier. While there's still a long way to go, our current successes pave the way for other entrepreneurs to step in and take our economic accomplishments to the next level.

Of prime importance—talk to other entrepreneurs who look like us and find out how they did it. If you already have hard-won experience, be a mentor. This is the single most important thing we can do for each other and for our socioeconomic status. Let me emphasize that—be a mentor. BE A MENTOR. It is through mentorship that we can change the landscape of our community. And while it's been some years since people in general have discussed apprenticeship, it's a concept worth bringing back to the fore.

The apprenticeship method of training works in favor of everyone involved. It can help those who are greenhorns in the field they love to gain invaluable experience that can help them flourish in the business world. Most business owners are so focused on competition that apprenticeship has all but died. But competition is nothing new. Take on an apprentice and teach him or her how to do what you do. This is how a new Black Wall Street or Rosewood can be created.

The community cannot thrive with just one grocery store, one clothing store, and one gas station. Build it by teaching up-and-coming entrepreneurs, so that there can be 21 theaters, 21 grocery stores, 21 gas stations. As you allow for expansion, your population will grow and begin to expand beyond just 10 blocks to 100 blocks. The more businesses, the more consumers you invite. In time, that new Black Wall Street or Rosewood will surface. Let apprenticeship be the medium for inviting fresh talent into your community.

Our strides have been incredible. We are a resilient people who need to keep pushing forward and never give up. The keys to success individually and collectively are simple: listen, learn, grow, adapt, teach, share, and mentor. Pay your rewards forward and take on an apprentice. Don't wait for them to find you—seek them out. Share your knowledge!

BLACK BUSINESS IN AMERICA

The number of black businesses in America is small relative to both the black and non-black populations. Even so, these businesses have an incredible impact on the U.S. economy. *Black Enterprise*, one of the leading magazines that tracks African American businesses in this country, publishes the names of the top 100 black businesses in the U.S. These are listed by industry and include the revenue of the top businesses owned and operated by African Americans.

This listing comprises information on a wide range of enterprise: advertising agencies; auto dealers; financial services, including asset managers, commercial and investment banks, private equity firms; and other sectors, including industrial/service companies.

According to *Black Enterprise*, GlobalHue topped the list of advertising agencies with $483.5 million in revenue. RLJ McLarty Landers Automotive Group brought in $541.7 million. World Wide Technology, in the industrial service sector, brought in $2.2 billion. These are the three businesses that brought in the most revenue. Entrepreneurs have 97 other businesses on this list alone to look to as role models for their future. Keep in mind that these 100 businesses are only the top of the list. There are all the other thousands of incredibly successful businesses that have produced not only wealth for their owners but employment opportunities for the community.

Black businesses contribute significantly to the U.S. market. Their participation is part of the fabric of America. In important ways, African American labor built this country. Black businesses are merely one expression of a hard-working people destined to reclaim our place in American society and culture.

BLACKS IN BUSINESS—BEFORE AND AFTER OBAMA

While some blacks prior to the Obama administration were experiencing relative success in business, many still believe there is a long way to go. With a black president in the White House, many expected a huge paradigm shift in the nation. Yet since President Obama took office, there has been a push to downplay any differentiation in how black businesses are handled compared to white ones. The debate goes on, as black businesses face many of the same difficulties as non-black businesses in a challenging economy. However, black businesses continue to fail at a far greater rate than non-black businesses. How can our firms survive in this contracted economic climate?

The debate may continue but the truth sits quietly on the sidelines—much work needs to be done. This is not only a responsibility shouldered by the business owners, but also by black consumers who could shift the course of African American businesses by supporting them and allowing the dollar to circulate longer in our community.

Is there a light at the end of the tunnel? I believe there is. Together we can transform the landscape of business for blacks in America by committing to a common goal: success.

WHY BEING A BLACK ENTREPRENEUR MAKES DOLLARS AND SENSE

CHAPTER 3

THE NEW ECONOMY

Figures are flying all over the Internet on the unemployment rate for blacks. While various agencies track African Americans collecting unemployment—the numbers range from 15 to 25 percent, depending on the source—no one tracks those whose unemployment compensation has run out. No one tracks those who can no longer receive unemployment and are now unsupported—or destitute.

So how do we ascertain the true level of unemployment among blacks?

We need to look at the already horrific variation of unemployment among different groups. For years, unemployment among blacks is almost always nearly double that of whites, as assessed by population and percentage. Now add those no longer receiving benefits—who are not counted—and the picture becomes bleak.

Even some of the most mundane jobs, such as factory work, are barely available, to blacks or anyone else, because much of our manufacturing has been sent overseas, with no sign of returning. The federal government doesn't seem to have any intention of managing the complete outsourcing of the many products that were once made in America. Mass production has won over quality production that once served the nation well. More than 75 percent of products sold on our shores are not made in America. Look around your home. Examine every item. How much of what you're looking at was not made in America, including your food and clothes. Even American-made cars are weighted down with foreign-made parts. Virtually no consumer item of consequence is made here any longer. And people wonder why the economy is taking such a severe downturn. The current economy is the inevitable end-product of several trends that have drastically altered the country over the last several decades—deregulation, outsourcing, and jobs migrating overseas.

Today, corporations are whispering to employees about their comfort level with moving to India to work. Others are being winked at with an offer of higher pay slipped to them on a folded piece of paper—and told that China isn't so bad. The hardest part will be learning a new language. Employees who once thought their federal and state jobs were safe havens are now realizing that the age-old belief that the government rarely fires anyone is now obsolete. Everywhere we turn, the American dream is being transformed, almost surreptitiously, into the Asian dream.

Welcome to the new normal.

Black employment trends may appear bleak. But necessity is always the mother of new intentions and new inventions. Becoming an entrepreneur in these transitional times could literally be a lifesaver. Finding an entrepreneurial niche that can rebuild business in America will be the boost the economy needs—even more so it is what the black community needs.

KEEPING YOUR BUSINESS RELEVANT AND MEANINGFUL

If you want to remain relevant, you must remain vigilant. More than just round the clock labor, it means taking the time to continually research your market to see what's changing and finding a way to change with it. Adaptability is of primary importance in the world of business. Life is fluid. The needs and desires of the population change over time. If you own a clothing company and imagine you can now make bell bottoms, you'd find yourself out of business before you can swipe a credit card. As the needs and desires of consumers change, you must be nimble and adapt your business.

When it comes to tracking current social trends—be vigilant. What are young people flocking to? What's going on with Gen X and Gen Y? How has retirement changed over the last few years with the stock market volatility? And what is the sixty-is-the-new-forty wave of seniors getting into these days? Know your local market and also monitor and respond to the changing global market. How can you expand your business to meet global needs? How have music, fashion, food, etc., changed accepted cultural trends?

When it comes to tracking the movement of the dollar—what's your money doing? Is it multiplying or declining in value? You may need to make adjustments based on the value of the dollar, not only in terms of the greater economy, but also because of shifts in your industry. Know how the value of the dollar affects service-oriented businesses compared to product-oriented businesses.

When it comes to understanding cultural moods—is it a time of peace or war? How does the current economic or environmental climate affect your business? The spirit of the culture can have a vast effect on your business. It can be what makes or breaks you. Know what changes are going on in the minds of your clients and potential clients.

CREATE YOUR OWN OPPORTUNITIES

Don't wait. Go to the mountain, because the mountain certainly won't come to you. One of the most amazing things about most entrepreneurs is their creativity. Many of the greatest inventions on earth were created by entrepreneurs—a single person or small group with a dream. How many ideas were scoffed at while they were being developed? You can bet hundreds. Entrepreneurs are some of the most creative people around. Is it because they're more intelligent than others? Certainly not. Many times it's all about survival. As Nelson Mandela says, "It always seems impossible, until it is done." Entrepreneurs are always reinventing themselves. This practice must always be nourished. Create, create, create. Never stop manifesting new opportunity. Complacency is the smother of invention. Building a business is a huge step, but maintaining that business can be just as time-consuming and challenging, particularly in a fluctuating economy.

THE MARKETING AND SELLING OF BLACK CULTURE

Remember the old Ray Charles commercial for Pepsi? "You've got the right one baby, uh-huh!" Jingles definitely sell. But jingles that cater to a particular group sell even more. Like the Ray Charles Pepsi commercial, more and more companies are using hip-hop to sell their products. Recently there was a commercial in which a bunch of mice in hip-hop gear are strutting down the street to a hip-hop tune. "You can get with this, or you can get with that!" "This" is a brand new car. "That" is a washer, drier, or other household item that cannot equal the luxury of a new SUV. The mice are shown riding in the appliance versus riding in the sporty green SUV.

Hip-hop culture has become the cash cow for many corporations. Like rock 'n' roll or Motown back in the day, it has impacted the minds and lifestyles of young people all over the country—and the world. It doesn't matter who does the singing when a subculture goes mainstream—the younger demographic—black, white, brown, yellow and red bounce to the beat. Global businesses know who the real consumers are, and they're making sure they cash in on the market by catering to those under the age of twenty-five. From Usher's protégé superstar heartthrob Justin Bieber to Snoop Dogg hanging with Martha Stewart or luxury goods like Cristal to Escalades promoted by the hip-hop legends corporations are making a killing. Hip-hop culture doesn't discriminate. In fact, it has a huge trendsetting appeal in the non-black community, making it a global market phenomenon in ways that couldn't have been anticipated twenty years ago.

Hip-hop sells, and it sells big. Black culture has been packaged and sold to the world on a global media-driven silver platter. Yet, too often the black community does not reap the rewards of this immense empire. Hip-hop, once regarded as a contemporary sub-culture that defined new music, fashion, slang and culture, turned 30 years old in 2004.

Journalist and cultural commentator Greg Tate offered an insightful analysis in "Hip-Hop Turns 30" in the Village Voice and why its cultural currency matters.

> The bitter trick is that hiphop, which may or may not include the NBA, is the face of Black America in the world today. It also still represents Black culture and Black creative license in unique ways to the global marketplace, no matter how commodified it becomes. No doubt, there's still more creative autonomy for Black artists and audiences in hiphop than in almost any other electronic mass-cultural medium we have. You for damn sure can't say that about radio, movies, or television. The fact that hiphop does connect so many Black folk worldwide, whatever one might think of the product, is what makes it invaluable to anyone coming from a Pan-African state of mind. Hiphop's ubiquity has created a common ground and a common vernacular for Black folk from 18 to 50 worldwide. This is why mainstream hiphop as a capitalist tool, as a market force isn't easily discounted: The dialogue it has already set in motion between Long Beach and Cape Town is a crucial one, whether Long Beach acknowledges it or not.

So much time has passed that many of us have forgotten that hip-hop was a positive movement meant to be a spiritual emancipation of the black community. Those who grew up in the late 70s and early 80s understood what hip-hop was. It was a new way of looking at the world—blacks telling true stories of our struggles, of our lives and what being black really meant.

The capitalization and commercialization of hip-hop has led to its fall from grace and today it is oftentimes used as nothing more than a means to fulfill the American capitalist fantasy. But authentic hip-hop is more than capitalism. It's emancipation. It's freedom. It's our oral lore, our history. Some who lived through the birth and growth of hip-hop might wonder—*where has it gone?*

Hip-hop has almost set up shop in Beverly Hills. It's time we shift the current trend and let hip-hop return to representing those who created it. Black culture and black businesses need to take back hip-hop, repackage it as it was meant to be presented, and give it to our youth in a way that restores it to its once-glorious genius, innovative and deeply entrepreneurial position.

THE BLACK BUSINESS AGENDA IN THE AGE OF OBAMA

Black businesses are struggling but it doesn't need to be this way. It's incumbent on business owners to look to each other for support. No business is an island. It's through collective exchange that African American businesses will thrive. In this age of Obama, many believe that the possibility of a new day has dawned. Others are still waiting for the sun to come up. No matter what you believe of this new age, it cannot be disputed that blacks are still in need of remedies for their business ailments. This book hopes to be a salve that will help black business heal and bring it to a new level. My goal is to help new entrepreneurs get their operations off the ground, assist new business owners by sharing ideas on how to stay afloat, and revive businesses currently on life support. The journey won't be easy. But is there anything worth truly having that comes easy?

TEST YOUR ENTREPRENEURIAL MUSCLES

Starting a business is easy. Anyone can do it, and it can be done within a day or two. However, starting a business that will survive involves more than just filing for trademarks and patents, and registering for a business license. In addition to these actions, you must plan carefully and execute strategically, if you are to avoid common pitfalls that can stop your business before it starts-up.

The following assessments will help you determine if your business aspirations are realistic. Starting a successful and sustainable small business will depend largely on your ability to map out a practical plan with a solid foundation. You must identify your vision, and be willing to work hard and to make the sacrifices necessary to make your dream a reality. This may require that you gain new technological skills or create your own mini-MBA program through online learning, good mentorship, or apprenticing in the field that you aspire to work in. Along the way you will need to develop a strong working knowledge of finance, marketing and pr, sales, management, bookkeeping, and market analysis. Mastering these basics is absolutely essential if your goal is to build a successful and profitable business and avoid unnecessary failure.

SO YOU WANT TO BE AN ENTREPRENEUR

Owning your own business sounds exciting, right? Who hasn't dreamed of being Donald Trump or being the winning candidate on *The Apprentice*? Nevertheless, it's time to inject some reality into your fantasy by responding to the questions in the following inventories.

Why do you want to be an entrepreneur? Check all of the reasons that apply.

- ☐ Freedom and independence—no boss can tell me what to do.

- ☐ A flexible work schedule.

- ☐ Unable to find employment.

- ☐ Currently underemployed and need additional income.

- ☐ Hit a dead end in my current job or field.

- ☐ Have an innovative product or service that I want to bring to market.

- ☐ Want to establish myself as a successful business person.

- ☐ Want to save for my retirement or retire early.

- ☐ Love the challenge of turning good ideas into profitable realities.

DO YOU HAVE WHAT IT TAKES?

Being an entrepreneur isn't for everyone. To decide if you really have what it takes, i.e. the entrepreneur's gene, answer the questions below honestly. A failsafe mechanism is to ask a close associate answer these same questions about you and your business skills.

	YES	NO
Are you naturally competitive? Do you like to win?	☐	☐
Do you enjoy making tough decisions?	☐	☐
Do you have a good imagination?	☐	☐

	YES	NO
Do others seek out your opinions when making important decisions?	☐	☐
Would you describe yourself as a natural leader?	☐	☐
Are you a good planner?	☐	☐
Can you connect the dots between cause and effect?	☐	☐
Are you able to get along well with a wide variety of people?	☐	☐
Do you adapt to new situations, people and unexpected demands easily?	☐	☐
Do you rebound rapidly from stressful demands, mistakes, and/or failures?	☐	☐

ENTREPRENEURIAL INTELLIGENCE

Business start-ups can demand extraordinary amounts of time and energy. The questions below will help you figure out whether or not you have the physical, emotional, mental, and financial intelligence required to start a new business.

	YES	NO
Do you have a strong physical constitution?	☐	☐
Are you capable of wearing multiple hats and working 24/7 if necessary to get the job done?	☐	☐
Are you emotionally mature and resilient?	☐	☐
Can you withstand cycles of intense pressure without falling apart or taking your stress out on others?	☐	☐

	YES	NO
Are you capable of making financial sacrifices and postponing short term gratification to build your business?	☐	☐
Can you operate without a financial safety net?	☐	☐
Are you willing to take calculated personal risks to take your business to the next level?	☐	☐
Do you regard business failure as an inevitable part of the business success cycle?	☐	☐

BASIC BUSINESS SKILLS

Starting and maintaining a successful business requires general and specific skill sets and experience. Learning how to accurately assess your general aptitudes is important so that you can eliminate your entrepreneurial weaknesses and rapidly turn them into strengths.

Are you a natural born salesman? An amazing inventor? A cost-cutting, make-something-out-of-nothing genius? Unparalled in your ability to put together a winning team? These basic business skills can be developed but first you have to know where you stand.

Entrepreneurial business skills can range from product invention, buying and selling abilities, economic forecasting, to executing pr and advertising campaigns. What's important to recognize is that developing basic business skills is not a random exercise or a guessing game. These are competencies that can be gained—but you must be willing to develop them. And the first step is to be willing to examine what you do know and what you don't know.

The questions below are a great jump off point for learning what skills you already possess and what action plan may be required to develop the skills necessary to get you where you want to go.

	YES	NO
Have you ever taken any basic business courses?	☐	☐
Have you ever sold new products or services?	☐	☐
Have you ever worked in a customer service department?	☐	☐
Have you ever produced a public event with direct ticket sales?	☐	☐
Have you ever been responsible for basic bookkeeping and/or inventory control?	☐	☐
Do you have hands-on experience in your proposed business arena?	☐	☐
Do you regularly read books, subscribe to newspapers, magazines, social media, or blogs in your business arena?	☐	☐
Do you actively seek out the latest trends and product innovations in your field?	☐	☐
Have you ever hired, supervised or trained new staff members?	☐	☐
Have you ever downsized, laid off, or fired anyone?	☐	☐
Are you willing to invest in additional education or training to develop basic or new business skills?	☐	☐

FINDING YOUR BIG IDEA

As business consultant Phyllis S. Quinlan once said, "You should always keep in mind that there's opportunity in chaos." Is there something you see that's broken that needs your special talent to fix? Coming up with a good idea is fairly easy, but great difficulty lies in finding a good idea that is feasible and realistic for you. There are hundreds of thousands of business ideas, but only one or a few will fit you. It's important to get this part right—if you pursue the wrong idea, you'll waste a lot of time, energy, and money.

The following questions will help you find your perfect fit—the business idea that has your name written all over it.

Describe the business that you plan to start. What was the seed or source of your business idea?

_____

_____

_____

What product or service will your business sell?

_____

_____

_____

Is your product an innovation or an evolution of an existing product?

_____

_____

_____

Is there a genuine market demand for your product or service? Does it fill a critical need?

_____

_____

_____

When compared on the basis of quality, price-point and accessibility is your product designed to compete with others in its field?

_____

_____

_____

Are you in business for love or money or both?

_____

_____

_____

If you were to abandon your big idea tomorrow what would the world lose? What would you lose?

_____

_____

_____

DISCOVERING YOUR MARKET

Never assume that people will automatically buy what you're selling. Just because your friends and family think that you've got the perfect business idea, remember there is no substitute for genuine market research.

Always be willing to connect with your potential customers to learn if they need or want your product or service and always ask how much they are willing to pay for it. Always encourage customer feedback and listen carefully to what your customers are really saying. The more deeply you stay connected to your market, the better you'll understand how to analyze its needs, capture its attention, and deserve its loyalty. Consider the following questions to begin your basic market research.

What are the demographics and psychographics of your potential customers?

_____

_____

_____

How much will pricing affect your customers' willingness to buy your products or services?

_____

_____

_____

Where do your customers live? Is your business easily accessible to your primary customers?

_____

_____

_____

What are your preferred pr, marketing, and advertising vehicles for letting your customers know about your products and/or services?

_____

_____

Have you ever conducted an online or face-to-face survey with your potential customers? If so, name one unexpected thing you've learned.

STARTUP

CHAPTER 5

SHOW ME THE MONEY

Are you ready to leave the comfort zone of your big idea and do what it takes to turn your good idea into a real business? Before you take the final leap forward it's time to contemplate one of the toughest challenges that every entrepreneur must wrestle with—the money question.

One of the most common reasons that businesses fail is due to insufficient funding. Just like you can't run a car without gasoline, you can't launch a business with out sufficient capital. So after you've identified the primary products or services that you want to sell to customers, it's time to take a deep breath and figure out exactly where your finances stand. Start by answering these basic questions.

How much money do you actually have on hand? What are your basic assets and liabilities?

My Money: Assets

_____, 20___

Cash on hand	
Savings account	
Real estate	
Automobile/other vehicles	
Investments (stocks, bonds, etc.)	
Total Assets	

My Money: Liabilities

_____, 20___

Monthly expenses (recurring bills)	
Mortgage or real estate loans	
Taxes	
Personal loans	
Credit card debt	
Other liabilities	
Total liabilities	
Net worth (assets minus liabilities)	

Now that you've taken a no-holds barred look at your basic finances and hopefully calculated a positive net worth, you're ready for the next step. Let's explore how much money you will need to start your business?

If you're really serious about succeeding in business, it's wise to have enough money to cover your first six months of operation. But in order to know what that price tag will look like you need to estimate your basic business start–up costs and your monthly overhead expenses.

Remember the goal at this stage is to get you to think like an entrepreneur. Before you invest energy in writing your business plan and upending your life or the lives of those near and dear to you, I want you to get comfortable with thinking about your money realistically.

So let's look at some basic business start-up costs. These costs may vary a great deal depending upon whether you're considering a retail business, a home-based business, or an online enterprise. The most important thing is to get comfortable with your money. Money represents energy and the more energy you have, the more energy you can create. Recognize that there is a great deal of truth in the statement that you have to spend money to make money.

THE START-UP

It's time to contemplate your basic business start-up costs and monthly expenses. For this exercise, just make your best cost guestimates and fill in the chart below. Remember this is all a warm up for your final business plan but taking the time to consider these questions now will help you "get your mind right." Practice really does make perfect, especially when you're launching a new business.

Basic Business Start-up Costs

Office lease, rental fees, or security deposits	
Furnishings and basic office equipment	
Installations (fixtures, equipment)	
Utility deposits (heat/air, water, and phone)	
Insurances	

Licenses and permits	
Legal or professional service fees	
Services and supplies (cleaning, accounting, etc.)	
Starting inventory cost	
Advertising	
Unanticipated expenses	
Total start-up costs	

Basic Monthly Business Expenses

Employee payroll and payroll taxes	
Employee health insurance	
Office rent and liability insurance	
Utilities	
Advertising	
Inventory	
Bank service and credit card fees	
Office expenses	
Repairs and maintenance	
Delivery/transportation	
Your salary	
Other	
Total expenses	

Now that you've determined your basic start-up costs and your monthly overhead, you will have a much more realistic sense of how much money you will need to meet your monthly business expenditures. This is a critical exercise because without this information you are playing at the idea of being in business but ill-prepared to launch and maintain one. Being in business requires a viable plan and the wherewithal to actually meet your monthly expenses and generate a profit.

CASH FLOW

Your ability to actually generate revenue from the sales of your products or services is called cash flow. That's why it's so crucial to determine what your monthly expenses are and if you can consistently generate enough income to cover your monthly costs.

Cash flow in any business is always subject to seasonal adjustments. A florist may experience a spike in business during popular holidays like Mother's Day or during summer weddings but have almost no traffic in January or September. If the business owner has no plan to attract additional customers to adjust for seasonal fluctuations, the enterprise will be doomed from the start. That's why diversity of products and customers is so important. A thorough business plan which accounts for these variables is an essential element in your blueprint for success.

Cash Flow Forecast

	Month 1	Month 2	Month 3
Cash in bank			
Petty cash			
Anticipated cash sales			
Total receipts			
Total cash & receipts			
Monthly business expenditures			
Cash balance			

If you have any anxiety about your money and your business, make certain that you get the help you need. I highly recommend taking the time to explore some of the outstanding business start-up resources now available to aspiring entrepreneurs. Remember, there is no substitute for one-on-one business coaching from a seasoned professional.

BUSINESS START-UP RESOURCES— GETTING THE HELP YOU NEED

There are many different resources that can assist you during the start-up process. Some can be extremely helpful; others can completely waste your time. I've identified the best ones based on their usefulness, accessibility, and other factors.

Organizations

These organizations can help you create a viable business plan, connect with invaluable resources, and keep you motivated and encouraged on your entrepreneurial path.

National Association of the Self-Employed (NASE): represents thousands of entrepreneurs and provides day-to-day support, benefits, and consolidated buying power for small businesses. www.NASE.org

National Black Business Council: dedicated to the creation and advancement of African American and minority-owned businesses, its mission is to create and support programs that will close the economic and digital divides between minority and majority businesses. www.NBBC.org

National Black Chamber of Commerce: reaching 100,000 black businesses, it's dedicated to economically empowering and sustaining African American communities through entrepreneurship and capitalistic activity within the United States and via interaction with the black Diaspora. www.NationalBCC.org

Small Business Administration (SBA): created in 1953 as an independent agency of the federal government to aid, counsel, assist, and protect the interests of small business concerns. www.SBA.gov

Small Business Training Network (SBTN): a virtual campus sponsored by the SBA that offers online courses, publications, and other forms of technical assistance. www.SBA.gov/training

SCORE: America's premier source of free and confidential small business advice for entrepreneurs. It offers advice online and in person at one of their 364 offices nationwide. www.SCORE.org

Minority Business Development Agency (MBDA): the only federal agency dedicated to advancing the establishment and growth of minority-owned firms in the United States. www.MBDA.gov

National Minority Supplier Development Council (NMSDC): provides a direct link between corporate America and minority-owned businesses; it was chartered in 1972 to provide increased procurement and opportunity for minority businesses of all sizes. www.NMSDC.org

Your local chamber of commerce: an organization made up of local entrepreneurs and business owners who meet regularly for networking, presentations, etc. Research online or inquire locally to find the one most appropriate for you.

Your local community's small business assistance center: there's a business help center in most cities, sponsored by the city, county, or state, that provides free services to aspiring and established business owners. Research online or inquire locally to find the one most appropriate for you.

SUPERSTAR ENTREPRENEURS

You don't have *to do* everything they say. You don't even have to agree with how they ran—or continue to run—their companies. But whether they're old or young, dead or alive, *you should listen to what they have to say.* I promise that you'll walk away from the one-on-one interviews that follow with at least one piece of knowledge that will benefit your company. Many of these multi-million dollar entrepreneurs had to overcome the same struggles that you now face.

BOB JOHNSON
FOUNDER OF BLACK ENTERTAINMENT TELEVISION (BET) AND RLJ COMPANIES

DL: What's your definition of a successful business?

Mr. Johnson: My definition of a successful business is one that creates value for all of its stakeholders and contributes to the economic growth of the broader society. By stakeholders, I mean all participants and beneficiaries of the business—this would include shareholders and employees; vendors and affiliates; service providers; customers and the community where the business resides. When you combine the contribution that a business makes to all of these stakeholders it should undoubtedly result in greater economic opportunity for the society at large.

DL: Who or what inspired you to be an entrepreneur?

Mr. Johnson: I don't know what makes an entrepreneur. I don't think you can teach it in business school or train someone to be an entrepreneur. It's something of an innate talent or desire that one has to pursue business opportunities, take risks, and have the self-confidence and motivation to pursue the creation of a value.

There are always people who encourage you in your entrepreneurial endeavors. Personally, I'd have to give the most credit for inspiration to John Malone, who at the time I started BET was the CEO of a large cable company and the principal investor in the BET start-up. He gave me what most entrepreneurs really need, and that was the encouragement that you can achieve whatever you want if you first believe in yourself.

DL: What's the number-one quality or trait that ambitious entrepreneurs overlook or underestimate?

Mr. Johnson: I don't believe there is such a thing as an ambitious entrepreneur. I think entrepreneurs are who they are because they believe there are no boundaries to opportunities. Their ambition is to achieve the best that they can in the pursuit of creating value in the form of service or product. If they overlook anything, it is probably the demand or the toll being an entrepreneur might take on their personal life or professional friendships.

Entrepreneurs have to master the essence of tradeoffs. Once they're able to find that core balance between their entrepreneurial goals and the joy of life, I think they're some of the happiest people on the planet.

DL: What's the most fatal business mistake you've ever made and what did it teach you?

Mr. Johnson: I don't believe in the idea of "fatal business mistakes." There are business strategies that may not achieve their ultimate goal; there are personnel decisions that may not be right for the particular assignment; and there may be investments that don't yield the desired return—but business is always about appropriate risks and appropriate rewards. The idea that decisions are "fatal" is not consistent with the idea that all business has risks. If you make a mistake you try to correct it and keep looking for other ways to achieve your objective. Clearly, there are some businesses that you can undertake that don't achieve their stated goals, but it doesn't necessarily mean that going into that particular business was a mistake. It could simply mean financial conditions weren't right, management was not appropriate for the demands, or that the overall economic model had challenges. Can these factors be fatal to a business? Absolutely, but it should not deter you from pursuing risks with the same commitment that first led you to become an entrepreneur.

DL: What have been the most vital steps in building your brand?

Mr. Johnson: The most vital step in brand building is creating a consistent commitment to quality, integrity, and strategic partnerships. In short, you are measured by the quality of your performance, not your personality, not your ethnicity, but rather by providing value and quality in what you do. Integrity is perhaps the most important asset that any person, whether in business or not, can have associated with their name. There is no substitute for character in business dealings or in life. I have deployed both integrity and quality value creation in building relationships with strategic partners. And each time those partnerships create value for each other it simply enhances the brand and extends the relationships that you have throughout the business community.

DL: How would you describe your business management style?

Mr. Johnson: My business management style is to have a vision about what opportunities exist, where I can create value, and how to go about building a team of individuals who can help reach those goals. I align my interests with my management team. I provide support, whether it's in the form of capital, leadership, or relationships to help the team pursue our joint goals. I give my management group the respect and support to allow them to become leaders in their own right and I trust that their commitment to the business mirrors my own.

DL: How did you create the original capital for your company?

Mr. Johnson: The original capital was created by my own sweat equity and vision in the founding and creation of BET with the support of a half-million-dollar investment by the aforementioned John Malone.

GEORGE FRASER
BEST-SELLING AUTHOR AND FOUNDER OF FRASERNET
(LARGEST NETWORKING CONFERENCE FOR BLACK
PROFESSIONALS AND ENTREPRENEURS)

DL: What's your definition of a successful business?

Mr. Fraser: A successful business is when you find a need and fill it, add a recognizable value, and provide extraordinary service over a long period of time.

DL: Who or what inspired you to be an entrepreneur?

Mr. Fraser: I was born "wired" to take risks. I learned my work ethic from my parents. And I've never seen anything as a "problem," only as an "opportunity." Those three attributes inspired me to pursue entrepreneurship only after I learned the business of business on someone else's dime—Encyclopedia Britannica, Procter & Gamble, and Ford Motor Company. I strongly recommend that for any aspiring entrepreneur.

DL: What's the number-one quality or trait that ambitious entrepreneurs overlook or underestimate?

Mr. Fraser: One: Work ethic. There is no day I don't work at least 12 hours. But it doesn't feel like work at all.

Two: The power and importance of relationships. Business is about relationships. Without relationships you have no business. Without relationships, you have no business being in business. In fact, the business you're really in is the business of building relationships.

DL: What's the most fatal business mistake you've ever made and what did it teach you?

Mr. Fraser: Trying to grow too fast. It put me into bankruptcy 15 years ago. The lesson I learned is you must have a large vision, but think small. Start small, build a success model, and then scale up over time.

DL: What have been the most vital steps in building your brand?

Mr. Fraser: Building a brand is like cooking in a crock pot—slow, long-term consistency produces a flavor to be remembered and loved.

DL: How would you describe your business management style?

Mr. Fraser: Management by walking around! I visit with and talk to my teammates in an inspiring, empowering, instructive, and humorous way. I manage with my heart, then head, but always with a smile.

DL: How did you create the original capital for your company?

| **Mr. Fraser:** | I used ALL my own money first, borrowed from close friends second, begged third. Until finally 10 years later I was able to walk then run. Today, I'm self-funded. |

EPHREN TAYLOR
CEO OF CAPITAL CITY CORPORATION (YOUNGEST BLACK CEO OF A PUBLICLY TRADED CORPORATION)

DL:	What's your definition of a successful business?
Mr. Taylor:	My definition of a successful business is one that makes an impact that is felt not only around the block, but also around the world. One that helps people elevate themselves to greatness. Our company focuses on making investments and launching products that help people become self-sufficient. I believe by helping people become self-sufficient I've positioned them with a lifetime tool that can then be translated to others. That's my small part to change the world.
DL:	Who or what inspired you to be an entrepreneur?
Mr. Taylor:	Not really a who, but a what. I believe a set of circumstances, and lack thereof, highlighted entrepreneurship as a viable option. Being from Carlisle, Mississippi, and being a black male in America presents enough obstacles of its own. I wanted to create my own destiny and not be dependent on someone else's system or job. I guess I started early, considering I launched a business at 12 years old selling video games I made on a school computer to my peers.

DL:	What's the number-one quality or trait that ambitious entrepreneurs overlook or underestimate?
Mr. Taylor:	Persistence. Entrepreneurs have gotten soft these days. Whatever happened to the knock on 100 doors till someone says "yes"? Even better, blow a hole through the wall! Nowadays, people want a "yes" like the speed of Google!
DL:	What's the most fatal business mistake you've ever made and what did it teach you?
Mr. Taylor:	Underestimating the power of marketing and not planning properly for success. Everyone plans for failure or worst case, but we rarely prepare ourselves for accelerated growth and the What if this really works? Success in our marketing almost killed our company. When you bring on that many new clients and that much money, the infrastructure will be put to the test. It taught me to always prepare for success.
DL:	What have been the most vital steps in building your brand?
Mr. Taylor:	Surrounding myself with talented, creative people who can set me apart from everyone else. Perception is reality, so might as well hire the best artists to paint that picture.
DL:	How would you describe your business management style?
Mr. Taylor:	I am a visionary. I hire generals to execute my battle plans. I believe in management by objective.

DL: How did you create the original capital for your company?

Mr. Taylor: I went out and asked for it the old-fashioned way. Banks have too much paperwork and ask way too many questions. I have a vision; I know how to get there. Are you in or not? Guess that's why a few million later I still get the "Yes!"

GWEN RICHARDSON
FOUNDER OF CUSHCITY.COM—
LARGEST AFRICAN AMERICAN INTERNET RETAILER

DL: What's your definition of a successful business?

Ms. Richardson: One that serves its customers, operates with integrity, and is able to make a profit.

DL: Who or what inspired you to be an entrepreneur?

Ms. Richardson: I was inspired by my father, who is a pastor (retired) and he also had many entrepreneurial endeavors at the church where we grew up. He was an innovator during the 1960s and 1970s, and opened one of the first church-run daycare centers in our area. He also opened a church-sponsored home for the aged, both of which are still in operation nearly 40 years later. I worked for him on a part-time basis during my high school years, and it just seemed better to be the boss than to be an employee.

DL: What's the number one quality or trait that ambitious entrepreneurs overlook or underestimate?

Ms. Richardson:	Integrity. People need to be able to count on your commitments and, if you cannot make them happen, let the person know.
DL:	What's the most fatal business mistake you've ever made and what did it teach you?
Ms. Richardson:	None has been fatal because all were learning experiences. As long as mistakes are not repeated, they're all part of the process. I think the most fatal mistake would be to quit before success is realized.
DL:	What have been the most vital steps in building your brand?
Ms. Richardson:	Consistency and determination. We have consistently promoted our business online for the 11 years since we started, week in and week out, without fail. And we didn't quit, even during the internet bust of the 90s and the recent economic downturn. Companies that survive economic downturns usually come out of them stronger.
DL:	How would you describe your business management style?
Ms. Richardson:	Detail oriented and hands off. I like to work with people who are self-starters and know what they're doing. Once the game plan is established, I prefer them to work independently, asking questions when things are unclear.
DL:	How did you create the original capital for your company?
Ms. Richardson:	We had an ongoing business and simply transferred the infrastructure to Cushcity.com,

which is essentially self-financed. But I've had investors too, and there's something to be said for both methods. When you accept venture capital, you have a lot more people to answer to—but you also usually have more resources to work with. When it is self-financed, you don't have those outside entities interfering.

TOM BURRELL
FOUNDER OF BURRELL COMMUNICATIONS—
GROUNDBREAKING AFRICAN AMERICAN ADVERTISING AGENCY

DL: What's your definition of a successful business?

Mr. Burrell: A business operation with an infrastructure, business culture, and institutional stability totally free of dependence on the presence of its founder, or any other individual for its life and perpetuation.

DL: Who or what inspired you to be an entrepreneur?

Mr. Burrell: Institutionalized racism.

DL: What's the number one quality or trait that ambitious entrepreneurs overlook or underestimate?

Mr. Burrell::   Humility. Embrace the notion that it is imperative to identify, attract, recruit, motivate, inspire, and retain people who can do a given job better than you can.

DL: What's the most fatal business mistake you've ever made and what did it teach you?

Mr. Burrell:	Over-reliance on standard measurements, symbols of achievement, such as advanced degrees from prestigious educational institutions, as a definitive indicator of competence.
DL:	What have been the most vital steps in building your brand?
Mr. Burrell:	Building a reputation for high professional standards, integrity, passion for what you're doing, as well as compassion for those you depend on to get the job done.
DL:	How would you describe your business management style?
Mr. Burrell:	Empowering. Forcing maximum growth through the delegation of responsibility, commensurate authority, and equivalent levels of accountability.
DL:	How did you create the original capital for your company?
Mr. Burrell:	The mail-order principal: "Don't spend what you don't already have." Get the order, collect the money, use some of the money to deliver the job, and put away what's left for taxes and net profits.

NADINE THOMPSON
FOUNDER OF WARM SPIRIT AND SOUL PURPOSE

DL:	What's your definition of a successful business?
Ms. Thompson:	It's actually quite simple for me: a successful business is one that is sustainable over time.

It must be self-sustainable, cash flow positive, and benefit its owner, employees, and the community to which it belongs, and most important be a source of pride for its owner and employees.

DL: Who or what inspired you to be an entrepreneur?

Ms. Thompson: First, my mother, who told me over and over again that having a business of your own and being self-sustainable is the only guarantee one has for independence. She said that you should not have to rely on someone else for a paycheck.

I was also inspired by the story and legacy of Madam C.J. Walker, who became America's first self-made millionaire, beginning with a career as an uneducated laundry woman. She also used direct sales, which is the same model that we use at Soul Purpose. She is a testimony to my mother's wisdom and the power of entrepreneurship. I incorporate all of these elements into my Soul Purpose business.

DL: What's the number-one quality or trait that ambitious entrepreneurs overlook or underestimate?

Ms. Thompson: The wear and tear, stress and challenges that come with success and growth. People think that growth is wonderful, but if you're undercapitalized or don't have an adequate plan to manage your growth it can kill you quickly. Cash flow management is extremely critical, especially during that time.

DL: What's the most fatal business mistake you've ever made and what did it teach you?

Ms. Thompson: Trusting a friend in business without a contract. The most important thing that I learned is that if a friend can give you their word verbally, they can also put their word in writing. It is simple and foolproof. A letter of understanding that each person drafts themselves and signs, and gives a copy to each other is a valuable piece of security against future misunderstandings, and at least keeps people true to their own word and their own understanding.

DL: What have been the most vital steps in building your brand?

Ms. Thompson: Making sure that the vision is written and communicated consistently, that the artwork and graphics are consistent with the vision. And finally, ensuring that the products and customer service are consistent with the vision and the promise.

DL: How would you describe your business management style?

Ms. Thompson: Collaborative and intuitive.

DL: How did you create the original capital for your company?

Ms. Thompson: My own savings, a small personal loan and one financial investor.

Farrah Gray
Youngest black to become a millionaire through business rather than entertainment

You may remember Farrah Gray as the young black entrepreneur who made his first million at the tender age of 14. Today, he now inspires thousands through his writing, consulting, and lecturing

He's probably best known as the author of the national bestseller *Reallionaire*. Now at 26 years old, Farrah Gray has a new book called *Get Real, Get Rich: Conquer the Seven Lies Blocking You from Success*. It debunks the seven common myths that people perceive as barriers to achieving their goals.

DL: What's your definition of a successful business?

Mr. Gray: To me, a successful, bona fide, money-making business is one that has a few things in alignment: your mission statement needs to be sound, and profitability must be there—but to be profitable you have to have the right team and the right vision.

DL: Who or what inspired you to be an entrepreneur?

Mr. Gray: I'm a strong believer that comfort is the enemy of achievement. So, I didn't know what entrepreneurship was, I just knew we didn't have any money. We were broke. So when you think of the entrepreneurial mindset, I call it "the third-world country mindset" because everybody there is born an entrepreneur. They don't have an Exxon, General Motors—they don't have those kinds of companies, so when you're born, you have to be an entrepreneur or else you don't eat.

A lot of people just start a business because it's going to be profitable. But as a small business entrepreneur, it's very important to have a passion for what you're doing. My first business, I didn't know it was entrepreneurship. I saw oversized rocks in the street and I started painting them. I would tell people "These are paperweights, bookends, and doorstoppers."

My mama always talked to me about money. A lot of times parents don't talk to their children about money—they don't have that Suze Orman or Glenda Bridgeforth conversation. My grandmother taught me that children are practicing adults, so give them the tools that they need.

DL: What's the number one quality or trait that ambitious entrepreneurs overlook or underestimate?

Mr. Gray: As for the person who wants to be an entrepreneur, I think some overlook knowledge. As it says in the scripture, people perish for the lack of knowledge. Understand your industry; you need to explore what will actually make your business tick. You need to look at your profit and loss statement.

Many African American entrepreneurs don't run businesses. Often our so-called business starts as a hustle for us, because we're trying to pay the rent, keep the utilities going, pay our car note. So we end up running it as a hustle as opposed to a business.

If you want to be an entrepreneur, don't overlook knowledge. It's important to acquire knowledge as it relates to writing a business plan and learning more about your business . . . not every business is going to be profitable in 3 – 5 years. However, you can write a business plan and dare yourself to be profitable within the first year. It's possible.

DL: What's the most fatal business mistake you've ever made and what did it teach you?

Mr. Gray: Just because you have money doesn't mean you have to spend it. When I first started out, I was a bit more frugal. But as you make more money, you tend to bring on more people, add expenses, and pay for things that, when you didn't have the money, you didn't have the option. So I think it's important to be as frugal as when you first started. And that's why there are major consulting firms that make millions of dollars just by consulting Fortune 500 corporations on cost-reduction strategies.

Why even focus on entrepreneurship with the economy as bad as it is? Firstly, you have to understand that 50 percent of Fortune 500 corporations that exist today were started in a recession.

DL: What have been the most vital steps in building your brand?

Mr. Gray: Bill Gates is known to have said, "If I had two dollars left, I'd spend one on PR." I find that, as entrepreneurs, we tend to forget that . . . many of us have to close our businesses because we . . . failed to advertise.

We wake up to an advertised alarm clock; we're in a bed that was advertised with sheets that were advertised to us. We take a shower, get dressed, and eat breakfast—all with products that were advertised to us. Then we get into a car that was advertised to us, walk into our business, and have to put a "Closed" sign on the door because we failed to advertise.

What has helped with *my* brand has been the fact that I let people know that I exist.

DL: How would you describe your business management style?

Mr. Gray: I really don't describe my style, I just believe in adapting and compensating.

DL: How did you create the original capital for your company?

Mr. Gray: I started off small. Really, I started an investment club with my friend on the south side of Chicago called "UNEEC," which is an acronym for the Urban Neighborhood Economic Enterprise Club. We were able to raise $15,000 through going to people who had more money than we had at that time, and that was pretty easy because that was pretty much everybody because we were kids. Then as we grew the funds to a $1.5 million venture capital fund, I went to higher net worth investors, which gave me the distinct honor, by God's grace, of being the youngest to have an office on Wall Street in U.S. history, then ultimately to become a millionaire. So I think, again, that I was able to do it by networking. I think your net worth has a lot to do with your networking skills.

WALLY "FAMOUS AMOS" AMOS
FOUNDER OF FAMOUS AMOS COOKIES AND CHIP & COOKIE

DL: What's your definition of a successful business?

Mr. Amos: A successful business is one that makes a profit for the investors, provides work for employees, that treats them with respect and creates an environment for their advancement, consistently offers the customers a quality product, and gives back to the community.

DL: Who or what inspired you to be an entrepreneur?

Mr. Amos: The word *entrepreneur* was not widely used when I started Famous Amos. I had been an agent at the William Morris Agency for seven years and a personal manager for another seven years, and was just tired of show business. I knew how to promote and bake a tasty cookie so it was inevitable that I would combine the two and sell chocolate chip cookies.

DL: What's the number-one quality or trait that ambitious entrepreneurs overlook or underestimate?

Mr. Amos: The power of teamwork. They think they can do it all by themselves. Big mistake. The only thing you can do by yourself is to fail. It's all about the team—together everyone achieves more.

DL: What's the most fatal business mistake you've ever made and what did it teach you?

Mr. Amos: Thinking that because I was "Famous Amos" I was the most important member of the team. The team is the most important. There is no "I" in team.

DL: What have been the most vital steps in building your brand?

Mr. Amos: Creating multiple exposures—television, radio, print, consistently having a positive attitude, giving back to the community through my work with promoting reading, being as visible as possible and consistently producing a quality product. Always being my best.

DL: How would you describe your business management style?

Mr. Amos: Finding the best person for the job, giving them the tools to perform at their best and letting them to the job.

DL: How did you create the original capital for your company?

Mr. Amos: I have started two companies: Famous Amos and Chip & Cookie. In both cases it was friends that put up the money. They invested in Wally Amos.

THE NEW GAME IN TOWN—SOCIAL ENTREPRENEURSHIP

While social entrepreneurship may be new to some, it is a very old system that has worked for African Americans for decades. As alluded to in previous chapters, Rosewood and Little Africa were created because of social needs that were not being met. These social needs gave rise to businesses that wanted to bridge the gap and create an environment that was socially supportive of blacks. And what better way than to create communities where we cater to each other?

What is social entrepreneurship? Amy Wilkinson, Senior Fellow at the Harvard University Center for Business and Government, and a Public Policy Scholar at the Woodrow Wilson International Center for Scholars, defines it as

> . . . practice of applying business and entrepreneurial principles to tackle social ills. For social entrepreneurs, success isn't only measured in dollar signs, return-on-investment is measured by return-on-impact as these innovative leaders build organizations for social good. And with impressive triumphs globally, social entrepreneurship is here to stay.

Andrea N. Johnson, Ph.D., of North Carolina A&T has been raising awareness about social entrepreneurship by putting its deep historical roots in the black community in context. "Social entrepreneurship has always been a part of the African American community. Although not always referred to as social entrepreneurship, businesses that create social value in the African

American community have always existed," says Dr. Johnson. "In order to continue the tradition of creating social value within our community, educational institutions such as Historically Black Colleges and Universities must lead the effort in educating future generations."

The growth of social entrepreneurship within our community has the potential to revolutionize the way African Americans do business. The utilization of entrepreneurial principles to heal social ills has had a huge impact on many communities around the world. Several African American social entrepreneurs have received attention for their ability to give something back to folks and encouraging the economic growth of the community by creating new businesses opportunities. Generating income and fostering self-sufficiency is essential to creating sustainable businesses. The following social entrepreneurs have, for years, been sharing their visions and offering their skills to free minorities from socioeconomic bondage.

MAJORA CARTER—GREENING THE SOUTH BRONX

The Boogie Down Bronx has long been known as a leader in hip-hop culture. But green was not one of its strong suits. With the many changes going on in the world, the Bronx is trying to bring back some of the foliage that had long been lost to concrete and asphalt. Majora Carter has been a huge part of this movement. As an environmental justice advocate and economic consultant from the South Bronx, Carter has been making waves. As the founder of the nonprofit environmental justice organization The Majora Carter Group, LLC, she has spearheaded the greening of the South Bronx.

Carter's interest in the socioeconomic status of Bronx residents did not begin yesterday. In 1997, while working for The Point Community Development Corporation as associate director, she advocated for the development of Hunts Point Riverside Park. Through a strong desire to beautify her hometown, she was able to secure a $10,000 grant from the New York City Parks Department as seed money. Through fruitful relationships fostered with community groups and the Parks Department, she was able to leverage that seed money into $3 million from the mayor's budget over a five-year period. The additional funding was used to build the park.

Prior to founding her current company, Carter founded Sustainable South Bronx (SSBx), for which she served as executive director until July 2008. It was through this organization that Hunt's Point Riverside Park was given new life after years of being coated with garbage.

Majora is a recipient of numerous awards and honors, including the Hollister Award; Liberty Medal for Lifetime Achievement; Paul Wellstone Award: Campaign for America's Future; Rachel Carson Award: National Audubon Society; New York State Women of Excellence Award: Lt. Governor David Paterson; Honorary PhD: Mercy College; and the Martin Luther King Jr. Award for Community Service.

Her achievements as a social entrepreneur are a testament to our ability to build—or rebuild—great communities that allow for improved social interaction and economic stability.

RUSSELL SIMMONS—"MTV MEETS DAVOS"

Russell Simmons is an empire unto himself. One of the major cultural forces of the hip-hop era, Simmons' contributions have spotlighted blacks and their ability to effectively participate in every area of contemporary culture.

As the founder of Def Jam, Def Poetry, and the fashion lines Phat Farm, Argyleculture, and American Classics, Simmons is a paradigm of industrious entrepreneurship. Under his corporate name, Rush Communications, Simmons has housed his management company, clothing companies, a movie production house, television shows, and an advertising agency. Less well known is his involvement in the David Lynch Foundation for Consciousness-Based Education and World Peace, as well as his practice in Transcendental Meditation and yoga. Simmons's charitable efforts are many. After Hurricane Katrina, Simmons and 22 top executives in the apparel and home fashion industries joined to form Fashion Delivers Charitable Foundation. Through this foundation, they donated new products to families in need who were victims of the hurricane. Simmons was also Goodwill Ambassador for the Slavery Memorial at the United Nations, appointed by U.N. Secretary General Ban Ki-moon. The appointment was to honor the victims of slavery and the transatlantic slave trade.

Simmons' social entrepreneurship has made a difference in ways some might not be able to imagine. Simmons's attendance at the invitation-only, Gen–Y-focused, $3,500 per head networking event, Summit Series conference, raises his social entrepreneurial skills to a new level. This summit invites some of the most talented in various industries, tracking innovations, business, altruism, personal growth, arts and revelry. An estimated 650 CEOs, authors, and start-up founders attended.

SHAWN JAY-Z CARTER—AFRICA "WATER FOR LIFE" PROJECT

Many regions around the world are experiencing a water crisis—the scarcity of good, clean drinking water. Music mogul Jay-Z chronicled his travels to the various regions affected by the water crisis while on his concert tour.

Jay-Z believes that it's not only important to use his voice for entertainment, but also to raise awareness. Youth are motivated by his campaign, with some taking action to support broad eco-friendly initiatives. His social entrepreneurship is facilitated by partnering with MTV and the U.N., which can use their influence and expertise to further the cause.

Nearly two million children per year suffer from lack of clean water and poor sanitation. By raising the awareness of people all over the world, Jay-Z hopes to model the kind of simple intervention necessary to make a life-changing contribution to children who suffer due to the water crisis. As Jay-Z says, "let's do some good!"

"Everything is a Business"

You should never say that you can't think of a business to start because everything around you is a business. The picture below is a snapshot someone may see while looking across the street, and it's loaded with many business opportunities.

- window cleaning
- siding replacement
- remodeling/construction
- brick laying
- air conditioning maintenance
- tree/plant grooming
- lock smith/door repair
- roofing
- gardening/lawn mowing
- tree stump removal
- signage
- awning cleaning
- restaurant
- window tinting
- selling tires
- auto detailing
- sidewalk repair
- auto repair
- water proofing
- drapery/blinds
- art gallery
- snow removal (in winter)

CHAPTER 8

ENTREPRENEURSHIP

THE BUSINESS OF BEING IN BUSINESS

Many people have the misconception that being successful in business means that you're a millionaire who lies around on the beach all day, doing nothing and collecting checks. The reality is that less than one percent of all business owners have this luxury. The average business owner reports to work every weekday to keep the business afloat, and according to a June 2010 survey by Payscale.com, small business owners can earn above average incomes, often topping $75,000 in the first year. Does this mean that they're not successful? Not at all.

Being successful in business is not based on how much money you make and how little you have to work. It's based on whether or not your business is really a business. In other words, if you're actually making money—you're successful.

Most people who start a business never generate a cash flow—let alone a profit. Most companies flop before they're even launched.

If you have a business that only makes $30,000 a year, don't be discouraged. You're on the road to success. You've been able to create some type of revenue—whether it supplements your income a little or a lot. Even a company that only generates $1,000 a year is technically successful. Millions of businesses have come and gone that never generated a penny.

Don't ever be misled into believing that your business is a failure because you have to work hard and don't own a yacht. The road to success begins with those first entries of actual profit recorded in your accounting ledger.

• ▣ • ▣ • ▣ •

HOW TO DISCOVER A UNIQUE BUSINESS CONCEPT

Okay—so you think every business idea out there has been done. You've looked through the phone book, online, and more. Everywhere you seek, someone is doing something you didn't think about.

What you may not realize, however, is that some of the best business ideas won't come from the Yellow Pages or the internet. Why? Because no one has thought of it yet, so it won't be found there.

Walk around your neighborhood. Take a slow, deliberate walk through your home. You could very well discover a new business idea by hanging out at the mall or visiting a local bookstore. Maybe sitting in the park or taking a stroll through the woods might unearth something you never imagined possible. Even simply cleaning out your closet might bring to mind something to assist folks in their homes.

Sometimes we feel that the competition is too great with many existing businesses, but unique opportunities are all around you. It may seem challenging at first to find something no one else is doing, but don't be daunted. The universe has a wealth of ideas at our disposal. One person can't think of everything.

Take your time, dig deep, and let an idea come to you. Use your surroundings to your advantage, and eventually something you never imagined might surface. You might be surprised to discover that those pesky little dandelions that we consider weeds are used for something very important today. Let your imagination soar. A new business venture could be on the horizon!

• ▣ • ▣ • ▣ •

How Do You Know When You Have a Good Business Idea?

Mark Cuban, billionaire owner of the Dallas Mavericks, once said that he knows when he's on to a good idea when everyone in the room *disagrees* with him. He feels that if no one else can see the logic in his idea, that proves how revolutionary and original his concept must be.

Many entrepreneurs, however, are quite the opposite. They feel they've discovered a good business idea when everyone around them can see the logic and *agrees* that they're on to something.

Of course, you'll never know if you have a good idea until you actually pursue it. It doesn't matter how many people agree or disagree with you. Only time will tell.

There are, however, some ways to determine whether or not your idea is realistic. If your idea turns out not to be realistic, then it's not a good idea. Here are three intriguing questions to ask yourself:

1. *Can my idea be easily duplicated?* Understand that you can patent a product, but not a service. If you come up with a unique service, you have to consider whether or not people can steal that concept from you.

   For instance, I remember having a conversation with a friend who had an idea about opening a unique store for women. She felt that whenever she went shopping for clothes, she could never find the right size—they would either be too small or too big. So she wanted to open a store with all half sizes (6 ½, 7 ½, and so on). Well, it wasn't a bad idea. However, if she pursued this and it became really successful—every clothing store nationwide would catch on and do the same thing.

   Her idea could be duplicated much too easily, and it would have backfired in her face if she went forward with it.

2. *How will I market my idea?* I know tons of people with great ideas, but when I ask how they'll market it, they get extremely quiet. Promoting a unique invention nationally costs money. Do you have those funds? Do you know how to raise capital? What about distribution? How will you get it into the stores? Will you sell online? Do you even know how that works? Be cautious about making the very costly and common mistake of creating a product, with little or no knowledge on how to let people know it exists.

3. *Will I be able to compete with bigger companies?* Keep in mind that patent protection doesn't last forever. Eventually, usually after 10 years, the patent for your product will expire and you cannot renew it. This means that other companies can take your idea. Will you be able to compete with them when this happens? Have you even considered this? If you don't think you can handle this, then your business idea is probably not a good one.

• ▣ • ▣ • ▣ •

USE THE TIME YOU HAVE

Stop viewing time as something that you'll never run out of. The reality is that you won't have forever to build your company. Stop procrastinating and use the time you have in this life to create your legacy. Learn to be an aggressive entrepreneur.

Did you know that more than 150,000 people worldwide die every single day? This means that in any given year, at least 5.5 million people will die from heart attacks, strokes, car accidents, household accidents, violent acts, old age—you name it. If you're reading this book, you're a survivor. You survived yesterday, last month, and last year. You should remind yourself of this every day and be inspired to become more productive.

Instead of laying around watching TV, use your free time to brainstorm, research, and plan. Instead of hanging out at bars, attend relevant networking functions to connect with the right people.

Instead of playing around on Facebook and BlackPlanet, visit the professional social networks, such as LinkedIn and Plaxo, to find yourself some valuable contacts. Instead of putting money away for vacations and cruises, save it to invest in your company to take it to the next level.

Recreation has its place, but right now it's time to build on those ideas that are in the back of your head. As an entrepreneur, you want to always pursue your business goals. It's not something you do every now and then—it's something you do every free moment. Most entrepreneurs aren't money-driven. Naturally, they do want to make money, but the real motivation is to have an impact on the world—to do something that would never have been done had they not been born.

If this sounds like you, then my advice is to stop fooling around. Use the valuable time you have to act on what will make you successful in business. Time goes on with or without you. Successful entrepreneurs understand this truth well and live by it.

● ▣ ● ▣ ● ▣ ●

CAN YOUR BUSINESS BE EASILY DUPLICATED?

Running a business that can be easily duplicated is dangerous. A competitor with more resources can come along, copy what you're doing, and then put you out of business. It happens all the time, and it's perfectly legal.

So what's the solution?

Well, unfortunately you can't just patent everything to protect yourself. The real solution is to lock it down. For instance, Wal-Mart does nothing more than buy items in bulk and sell them to customers at a discount rate. This is very simple, and should be able to be duplicated—but they've locked it down, making it extremely difficult for anyone to compete with them.

Here are five ways to lock down your product or service and prevent your business from being easily duplicated:

1. *Intellectual Property*

   Buy every domain name and register every trademark that's affiliated with your industry. Try to imagine what your competition might do, and do it before they do. For instance, if you own a car dealership in Greenfield, Colorado—you'll want to get GreenfieldCars.com, GreenfieldTrucks.com, GreenfieldCarDealership.com, etc. You'll also want to own the trademark for "Greenfield Cars," "Greenfield Car Deals," "Greenfield Car Discounts," etc.

2. *Branding*

   One reason why other companies can't compete with Wal-Mart is because their brand is too powerful. Wal-Mart is always running an extensive advertising and PR campaign. You should do the same. If your clients see your brand often enough and it meets their needs, they'll respect it and will not easily shift direction when a new competitor comes to town.

3. *Relationships*

   You must create and maintain close professional relationships with your clients. This can be done directly and indirectly. Your clients should be more than colleagues—they should be friends and family. They have to know that you care about their success. If they feel this way at all times, it'll be hard for a duplicator to come along and recruit them.

4. *Customer Service*

   Your customer service must be excellent and unique. Be different and creative, and offer your clients something they can't get elsewhere. Don't be greedy. Cut prices if you have to. This alone can make it nearly impossible for a duplicator to compete with you.

5. *Research*

   Always be in the habit of researching and brainstorming. Attend industry conferences and read industry publications. You should always know about the latest development in your industry, and you should never hesitate to make the necessary adaptation so as not to fall behind. If a duplicator comes along with a more modern approach, this could be very threatening to your company.

• ▣ • ▣ • ▣ •

THINK LIKE A RESTAURANT OWNER— PASS THE PROFITS, PLEASE

Restaurants are closing down all over the country. Many have been in business for years but are not able to weather the current economic storm. Like it or not, many are simply not using some basic strategies that would make a huge difference.

I have absolutely no interest in the restaurant industry nor any interest in ever owning a restaurant. However, if I did own a restaurant, here are some things I'd do to keep my business afloat:

1. *Eat free on your birthday.* Invite customers to eat for free on their birthdays because in most cases they'll be accompanied by family and friends who, of course, will pay to eat.

2. *Collect customer data.* Get the e-mail addresses, cell phone numbers, and mailing addresses of every customer who walks in your restaurant. With their permission, once a week I'd e-mail and/or text them coupons and specials. Also, once a month I'd snail mail them some type of promotional postcard.

3. *Just desserts.* Strongly encourage customers to order dessert while ordering their appetizers and entrées.

Many dessert orders are lost because customers are simply too full after finishing their food.

4. *Express dining discount.* If your restaurant is regularly crowded, offer customers 5 percent off their bill if they finished eating their meal within 30 minutes. This would enable you to serve more people, instead of turning people away or having them wait for an hour or more to be seated.

5. *Entertainment sells.* Offer entertainment (music, comedy, etc) with the meal. Research shows that people love to be entertained while eating and are more likely to come back if they are. There is always a good local band or musician out there eager to gain exposure and an audience for a reasonable price.

6. *Kids rule.* Offer "free kid's meal" or "free kid's dessert" coupons to the local elementary schools to distribute to students who excel. Kids will harass their parents about taking them to get their free food, and parents will likely buy something for themselves while there.

7. *Reward patronage.* Incentivize customers with a simple reward program. For every five meals offer a free meal worth the value of the average check. For instance, if you spent an average of $15 per meal, your sixth visit would include a free meal up to $15. This reward would encourage people to be regular customers.

8. *Carryout service.* Give all of your customers a refrigerator magnet that displays your restaurant's phone number and website. This will help them remember that they can order carryout on the phone or online.

These are just a few concepts that I'd introduce that I notice 90% of the restaurants I go to don't do. Whether you own a restaurant or not, don't ever allow your business to fail because you didn't implement some simple, easy, cost-effective ideas.

• ▣ • ▣ • ▣ •

BUSINESS LESSONS FROM O.J.

Most people had had enough of O.J. Simpson in the early 1990s when he was acquitted of killing his wife, and in 2006 when he wrote a book entitled *If I Did It*. However, it was Simpson's conviction for his stick-up robbery in Las Vegas that attracted my attention. He's been sentenced to up to 33 years in Nevada state prison, and isn't eligible for parole for nine years.

So what are the business lessons one can learn from O. J? Here they are:

1. *Don't Gamble*

    It's rumored that Simpson turned down a plea deal to do only three years in prison. He gambled and lost, and now he's facing more than 10 times the time.

    Gambling too can hurt entrepreneurs. Granted, being an entrepreneur is risky—but it doesn't mean that you should make reckless decisions. You should always be realistic with your expectations, and never ever turn down a reasonable deal.

2. *Be Honest and Ethical*

    Had Simpson been honest about retrieving his stolen items, he would have gone to the police. However, he didn't want the items to go toward the financial settlement that he owed the Goldman family. This dishonesty hurt his case badly.

    Entrepreneurs too should always be honest and ethical in their business dealings. Remember that what goes around comes around, and that tons of business owners are locked up every year for fraud, stealing, and/or running scams.

3. *Choose Your Business Associates Wisely*
   Another thing that hurt his case was the company he kept. While attempting to retrieve his belongings, Simpson didn't know that the individual who accompanied him had a gun. Several others he hung out with were convicted felons. This weighed heavily in his case.

   Entrepreneurs should be careful about being affiliated or associated with disreputable or questionable business people. They can hurt your reputation, which could lead to a drop in revenue. You also run the risk of being in the wrong place at the wrong time and finding yourself guilty of being an accomplice.

4. *Not All PR is Good PR*
   Simpson's harsh sentence was his own fault. Over the past 15 years, he has received some of the worst possible criticism from the media. Although it shouldn't happen, the media shapes our opinions— and the judge in his case obviously did not think very highly of him.

Entrepreneurs should remember that a very common misconception is that all publicity is good publicity. Not so. Remember this when planning your marketing strategy, and aim to get as much good PR as possible. One wise man put it perfectly: "Make the news, not the headlines."

• ▣ • ▣ • ▣ •

DON'T ASSUME—FIND OUT FOR SURE

It's a bad habit that entrepreneurs seem to fall into constantly. Instead of finding out for sure, we make assumptions. We typically do this because of time constraints, but be careful—this is one bad habit that can really hurt you in the long run.

For instance, suppose you're interested in exploring new marketing avenues. You've thought about postcard marketing or search-engine advertising, but you haven't moved forward because you don't *think* it will work. The truth is, you'll never know if it works until you find out for sure. Why not run a small test to see what happens? Invest $100 and a week's worth of time. If it works, it works. If it doesn't, it doesn't—but at least you'll know for sure.

Another example. Suppose you assume that all your customers and clients are satisfied with your company's services. You've thought about asking them, but you haven't done so because they *seem* to be happy. The truth is, you don't really know if your clients are happy until you ask them.

So, why not ask them? Send out an e-mail with a brief online survey or questionnaire. Or when speaking with them, ask: "Are you pleased with our services? How can we improve?" Maybe they're happy, maybe not. At least now you'll know for sure and can make enhancements if necessary.

Many times basic assumptions such as these will have you missing out on opportunities that you never knew existed, and losing opportunities that you never knew could be saved.

• ▣ • ▣ • ▣ •

ARE YOU A SERIAL ENTREPRENEUR?

There are two types of entrepreneurs. Both are risk-takers and both are driven. One, however, will start a business and quit if it fails. The other one will start business after business, until he finds one that works. The latter is called a serial entrepreneur. Does this describe you?

Clemson University professor Wayne Stewart took a close look at how serial entrepreneurs differ from their more traditional counterparts. In one study, Stewart and his colleagues concluded that serial entrepreneurs were bigger risk-takers, more achievement-oriented, and had a higher preference for innovation. "The results," he says, "suggest that there is a psychological profile that drives serial entrepreneurs, predisposing them to multiple venturing."

As for whether serial entrepreneurs are born or made, Stewart tends toward the former. While environmental influences, such as parenting, education and culture, do affect behavior, innate characteristics like leadership and intelligence manifest themselves very early on in life, he explains.

What is certain is that serial entrepreneurship is an extremely important economic and social phenomenon especially in a capitalist system. "Estimates are that about one-third of new ventures are initiated by serial entrepreneurs, and their firms tend to be larger," Stewart says, noting that higher business success rates may be attributable to prior experience and the resulting ability to leverage a wider network of key customers, suppliers, partners, and financiers—all crucial to business creation. The subject, he concludes, "deserves more research in order to provide better prescriptions for practice, and to facilitate policy that encourages entrepreneurial activity."

• ▣ • ▣ • ▣ •

20 BILLION HOT DOGS

According to the National Hot Dog and Sausage Council, Americans eat 20 billion hot dogs each year. That means we eat about 633 hot dogs per second. These astronomical numbers don't even include hot dog sales from Wal-Mart, sporting events, or street vendors—all of which do not disclose sales data.

What does this mean for you and me? Well, it means different things to different people. But one thing's for sure: Despite a recession, people are still eating, they're still spending money on food, and they're making food companies filthy rich.

If people are buying this many hot dogs, imagine how many hamburgers, loaves of bread, and cartons of milk are being sold. Imagine how many bags of chips, candy, and sugar are being sold.

What does this mean for entrepreneurs? The meaning will vary depending upon your passion and your expertise. Some entrepreneurs might consider getting into the food industry. The bottom line is that it's always a good time to explore unsung and potentially profitable business ideas.

• ▣ • ▣ • ▣ •

BLACK WOMEN, BLACK HAIR CARE, AND THE ECONOMY

The black hair care industry generates billions every year from products sold in stores, and from services provided in beauty salons. According to the Design Essential Mane Attraction Survey black women continue to make their hair a priority—even during a recession.

The survey reported in *Louisiana Weekly* via Target Market News revealed that the majority of African-American women base their salon and stylist choice on trust, cost, and time consumed. With the current economic contraction, affordable hair care is harder to find but black women have stayed committed to their beauty regimens.

Black hair care has always managed to fit into the budget. While some might assume hair care would be the first luxury to go, studies have shown that despite the present economic state of America and the prices at most salons, black women still flock to their hairdressers for routine maintenance.

"Some weekly clients have changed to every other week. But the majority of clients have been keeping up with their appointments," said Britney Adams, a stylist at New Image Salon in Harvey, Louisiana.

Shalonda Armstrong, Director of Marketing at Design Essentials commented, "…many African American women are opting to save money by doing their hair at home sometimes. Ultimately, a vacation may no longer be in the budget, but there is still room for the occasional trip to the salon."

For visionary entrepreneurs eager to serve a loyal market, black hair care products and services will always represent a growth market.

• ▣ • ▣ • ▣ •

Local Business vs. National Business

Anecdotal observation tells me that both local and national businesses have the similar advantages and disadvantages to consider. I believe either type is worth pursuing once you determine which is best for you.

- *A local business* serves customers and clients within the city or state in which the company operates. A firm that offers the following services would likely be a local business: carpet cleaning, plumbing, auto detailing, tax preparation, hair care, etc.

- *A national business* serves customers and clients across the country, and may even have offices in several states. A firm that offers the following services would likely be a national business: advertising, public relations, consulting, merchandise distribution, book publishing, etc.

Here are some thoughts on both:

1. A national business is best to pursue because there are many more people and thus more potential clients. While this much is true, at the same time it's much easier and cheaper for a local business to recruit clients. Recruiting clients nationally is much harder and more costly than a local effort.

2. A local business is best to pursue because it will keep your company smaller, and thus more stable to weather an economic storm. This may be true, but if the economic challenges are specific to your local area, you'll wish you had clients elsewhere.

3. A national business is best because you can grow into an empire, and one day expand globally. This may be true, but sometimes keeping it simple and small is smart—and less stressful.

4. A local business is best because it's easiest to establish a word-of-mouth marketing campaign. This may be true, but if a customer has a bad experience with your company, this will circulate very fast.

So, local or national—one is not necessarily better than the other. Consider the advantages and disadvantages, and decide which is best for you. Many entrepreneurs have decided to pursue both opportunities and have gained recession proof profits.

• ▣ • ▣ • ▣ •

FRANCHISE YOUR WAY TO FREEDOM

Opening a franchise is probably one of the most effective methods of starting a business. The start-up costs are fair, and everything needed to run the business is already in place. Many entrepreneurs want something that'll give them stability but find the research and work needed to get started so overwhelming that they often abandon their ventures even before they've begun.

In our current economy, a franchise that has proven to be financially viable is a good bet. Start a franchise and allow those who came before you and worked hard to build the business lay the foundation for your success.

One valuable resource for not only finding a franchise but also for helping you get the preliminary information you need to begin your venture is MinorityFranchising.com. This site provides a very exhaustive list of franchises for every kind of entrepreneur.

• ▣ • ▣ • ▣ •

ARE YOU A CONSULTANT?

Independent consultants have become the new BFFs of businesses both large and small. The need to know in today's business environment demands the best information in the most timely manner. What distinguishes a good consultant from a bad consultant is an outstanding knowledge base, a depth of experience, passion and a commitment to serve.

Do you have skill sets that mesh with the top 20 consulting businesses thriving in today's economy?

1. *Accounting*: A skilled numbers person is someone that every business needs, no matter how large or small. Accounting consultants can help a business with all of its financial needs.

2. *Advertising*: A necessary area for any business that wants to develop a good strategic campaign to let the world know what it offers.

3. *Auditing*: From professionals who audit utility bills for small businesses to those who handle major work for telecommunication giants, auditing consultants earn the respect they deserve.

4. *Business*: Know how to help a business turn a profit? If you have a good business sense, then you might excel as a business consultant. After computer consulting, people in this field are the next most sought after.

5. *Business writing*: Everyone knows that most businesspeople have trouble writing a report—or even a simple memo. Enter the business writing consultant, and everyone is happy!

6. *Career counseling*: With more and more people finding themselves victims of corporate downsizing, career counselors are in demand. They guide clients into a profession or position that will help them be both happy and productive.

7. *Communication*: Consultants who specialize in helping employees in both large and small businesses

communicate well with each other help iron out operational bumps and improve efficiency.

8. *Computer consulting*: From software to hardware, and everything in between, if you know computers, your biggest problem will be not having enough hours in the day to meet your clients' demands!

9. *Editorial services*: From producing newsletters to corporate annual reports, editorial consultants who are unsung content experts will always be needed.

10. *Executive search/headhunting*: People who enjoy discovering and marrying talent to the best possible employers fill an important function.

11. *Gardening*: In the past decade the demand for gardening consultants has blossomed (pun intended) into a $1 million-a-year business. Not only are businesses hiring gardening consultants—so are people who are too busy to take care of their gardens at home.

12. *Grantsmanship*: If you know how to write a grant proposal, you can generally name your price.

13. *Human resources*: As long as businesses have people problems (and they always will), HR consultants will be in demand for business clients, both large and small. The new workplace requires new skills from on-going education in new business systems to teaching employees mutual respect, to downsizing with legality and compassion. Wise counsel in the workplace is always needed.

14. *Insurance*: Everyone needs insurance, and everyone needs an insurance consultant to help them find the best plan at the best price.

15. *Marketing*: If you can help a firm write a marketing plan, or you have ideas that you believe will help promote a business, this type of consulting may be for you.

16. *Payroll management*: Everyone needs to get paid. By using your knowledge and expertise in managing payroll, you can provide this service to multiple businesses, both large and small.

17. *Public relations*: Getting good press coverage for any organization is an art. When an organization finds a good PR consultant, they hang on to them for life!

18. *Publishing*: A publishing consultant helps to launch new ventures—from a magazine, newspaper, or newsletter, to even a new website or electronic newsletter.

19. *Taxes*: With the right marketing and business plan (and a sincere interest in the field), your career as a tax consultant can be very lucrative by advising businesses on legal ways to pay the least amount of tax possible.

20. *Writing services*: Anything related to the written word will always be in demand. Find the right niche and you could be in big demand.

• ▣ • ▣ • ▣ •

STOP MAKING STUPID REMARKS

Too often I hear black entrepreneurs saying stupid things that get in the way of making money.

Here are the top four remarks that no one ever needs to hear you say:

1. *"I don't fly on airplanes."*
   What? You don't fly? What if you have to meet with a client face-to-face? What about business conferences?

Not flying on airplanes can be a great obstacle to your business success. If you want to be a successful entrepreneur, you need to get over your fear of flying. Do the research. It really is the safest way to travel. If you get airsick, then you need to invest in some Dramamine®, a popular over-the-counter medicine for motion sickness.

2. *"Banks don't give loans to black businesses."*
Wrong! While African Americans have experienced more difficulty obtaining financing than whites and other groups, there are banks that give loans to black companies all the time. Bank of America, Chase, and Wells Fargo even have special programs designed to help African American entrepreneurs. And the federal Small Business Administration has several loan programs for blacks.

   The reason you can't get a loan may be because your credit is jacked up! If that's the case, you need to fix your personal credit and re-approach your bank about establishing a business line of credit. You'll almost certainly get a different response.

3. *"This business is going to make me rich overnight."*
Having a good idea doesn't guarantee that you're going to instantly attain wealth. Any successful entrepreneur will tell you that it takes at least twelve to eighteen months to make money from a good idea. In most cases, true profitability can take from three to five years. Getting excited or overly anxious about get-rich-quick fantasies makes you look and sound immature or delusional. In addition, the gap between fantasy and reality will only discourage you when your naive dreams are not realized.

4. *"I don't do business with white people."*
That's the dumbest thing a businessperson could ever say, but some say this because they want to keep their

money circulating within our community. I'm all for buying and spending within the black community. But at the end of the day, to be successful you have to do business with the company that delivers the best product.

Support your community, but also support your company. You don't want your business to fail because you got caught up in some racial ignorance. Besides, there are services out there that you need that may not even be provided by a black-owned company.

It's been proven over and over again: companies that embrace diversity reap benefits beyond just their bottom lines. It took white companies years to realize this. Don't make the same mistake they did.

• ▣ • ▣ • ▣ •

BUSINESS BLUNDERS

Why do smart people make dumb business decisions? According to author and clinical psychologist Madeleine Van Hecke, the answer is simple—blind spots. In her book *Blind Spots: Why Smart People Do Dumb Things*, Van Hecke addresses a list of 10 mental glitches or blind spots that make very intelligent people do very unintelligent things.

Some of these include "not stopping to think," "not noticing," "jumping to conclusions," and "missing the big picture."

This kind of obscured vision makes me think of companies like BP or those financial executives at Washington Mutual and Wachovia who authorized subprime mortgage loans to families they knew couldn't afford the homes. It also includes entrepreneurs who invest a lot of money in their ideas without doing market research. Or those of us who fall victim to some product or service that guarantees results that we know are too good to be true.

Van Hecke confirms that *everyone* has blind spots and encourages people to embrace and understand their weaknesses to improve personal and professional decisions and relationships. This must-read book rated five-star reviews on Amazon.com, which declared it to be "a good book for business groups, or anyone wishing they didn't stumble over their own forehead-smacking blunders."

● ▣ ● ▣ ● ▣ ●

How to Achieve Financial Freedom

Everyone wants to be financially free. Yet the road to that freedom seems paved with a host of seemingly impenetrable obstacles. Many are created by our own fears. For instance, fear of success can drive us to do things that are self-defeating.

It is incumbent on us to recognize the role we play in delaying our financial success. Once that's discovered, all else is a matter of hard work and application. Making money is challenging, yes, but there are numerous factors that, if mastered, can make achieving financial success easier.

First, **take charge** of your business. It's important to know every aspect so you can effectively manage it. This is integral to ensuring your finances are in order and your money is working for you.

Next, **believe** that your efforts will be fruitful. Work very hard with the conviction that you're building value and personal wealth. In the short run, the wealth may not be monetary, but by building a reputation, the monetary wealth will begin to present itself.

Finally, **invest wisely**. Learning how to make your money work for you is key to building wealth. Invest only what you can afford to lose, never more. Stay on top of the changes in the market and keep your money circulating. Over time, you can build a mini-empire that will have you set for life.

Financial freedom is not as distant as it may seem. Stay the course and believe in your product or service. Don't let the naysayers steer you from your path.

• ▣ • ▣ • ▣ •

How to Be a Freelance Entrepreneur

Freelance entrepreneurs (or freelance workers) are self-employed individuals who pursue various professions without a long-term commitment to any one employer. Basically, they're independent contractors that get paid on a per-project basis.

Freelance entrepreneurs may be photographers, graphic designers, journalists, publicists, web developers, and even business coaches. Anyone with a skill in demand can be a freelancer.

If you're interested in freelance entrepreneurship, here are some great website tools:

- *Elance.com*—the number one online workplace where businesses find and hire people "on demand" to get work done quickly and cost-effectively. This is a great place for freelance entrepreneurs to list themselves.

- *FreeLancer.com*—the number two online marketplace for freelance entrepreneurs and companies looking to hire them. This is also a great place to list your profile.

- *iFreelance.com*—the number three online destination for freelance entrepreneurs and employers to interact. It would definitely be worth listing your profile here as well.

Being a freelance entrepreneur can be a very financially rewarding career. One great benefit is that you are your own boss. You can often work at home and set your own hours.

However, a major downfall is that you're responsible for keeping your work steady. You have to make sure that business is consistent so that your cash flow is constantly flowing. In addition, you have to file taxes as a business—which is very different from personal taxes.

For information on how to be successful as a freelance entrepreneur, it may be wise to join the Freelancers Union (freelancersunion.org), a non-profit organization that represents the needs and concerns of America's growing independent workforce through advocacy, information, and service.

• ▣ • ▣ • ▣ •

THE WEEKEND ENTREPRENEUR

Believe it or not, most entrepreneurs also have "day" jobs. They may be business owners but don't quite make enough to live. Many devote some hours each evening to their own business, but the bulk of their freelance time is spent on weekends.

Are you a weekend entrepreneur? If so, don't feel discouraged. This is completely usual and part of the process. Nearly every successful entrepreneur I can think of had to do this at one point, including myself. Keep at it, and don't give up.

Before you know it, you'll be a full-time entrepreneur generating enough revenue on which to live. Just remember to make the most of your time. Recreation is fine as long as you don't spend too much time hanging out and watching TV.

Develop a "work now, play later" attitude, and your business goals will be reached sooner than you might think.

• ▣ • ▣ • ▣ •

NEVER TOO LATE TO BE AN ENTREPRENEUR

According to economists and small business observers, the number of individuals starting their own companies during what is usually considered the "retirement years" is on the rise. BusinessWeek.com confirms that there are of tons of "older" people who are entrepreneurs.

The AARP Public Policy Institute reported in 2008 that 21 percent of the self-employed were between 55 and 64, while 10 percent were 65 and older. In the new economy we can be sure that this number will continue to increase. In fact, workers 50 and older are more likely than younger folks to own their own businesses.

According to the Ewing Marion Kauffman Foundation, a non-profit in Kansas City, Mo. Americans ages 55-to-64 have demonstrated the highest rate of entrepreneurship, leaving recent college grads and career changers in the dust. This news should be very motivational for those who are approaching 50, 60, or even 70—it's never too late to pull up a chair to the business conference room table. Entrepreneurship is wide open to anyone who has the passion and the drive to turn an idea into reality.

You're never too old to take the entrepreneur's journey. It starts with that ageless first step.

• ▣ • ▣ • ▣ •

NOW THAT YOU'RE AN ENTREPRENEUR, SHOULDN'T YOU BE RICH AND FAMOUS?

So you're a business owner or entrepreneur or author or expert. You've got clients, nice business cards, a few employees, and maybe some office space. Perhaps you've even been featured on TV and in a few magazines.

Colleagues see you as successful, but family and friends think that by now you should be rich and famous. They want to borrow money, and don't understand when you turn them down. Is that realistic? Should all entrepreneurs be living like celebrities with money to give away? If you aren't living large, does that mean you're doing something wrong?

Actually, the only people doing something wrong are the people who think in that manner. Being a successful entrepreneur does not mean that you have to drive a Mercedes Benz and live on million-dollar beach-front property.

Being a successful entrepreneur simply means that you've created a way to earn a living without working for someone else. Whether you've created full-time or just part-time income, you've far surpassed millions of individuals who attempt to start a business but generate no income at all.

You should celebrate the fact that you're even in the game, let alone in a country where there are business opportunities available for you. Don't be hard on yourself because you may not have reached celebrity status. The key is that you're still in business. Anyone who's figured out a way (legal and ethical, of course) to get others to spend money with you, has done far more than any family member or friend may ever realize. If you create a company that does nothing more than allow you to eat and pay rent, you're already a history maker and should be applauded.

Don't be complacent, though—I encourage you to reach for the stars. If it's your goal to do so, do all you can to become the next Bob Johnson or Bill Gates or Oprah Winfrey. But until then, give yourself credit where credit is actually due—and ignore those spectators who have no idea of the skill and energy it takes to start and maintain a business.

Entrepreneurship—Business Secrets

1. Work on holidays and weekends. While everyone else is goofing around, you should be working toward your business goal. Develop a "work now, play later" attitude.

2. Be a serial entrepreneur. Start business after business, pursue idea after idea until you find one that works. Never feel bad or ashamed when you fail—it's perfectly normal and will only make you wiser.

3. Don't settle for "almost." Almost doesn't cut it. Either you're going to see a venture through or you're not. There's no in-between. If you quit before you make it, you can never say you were an entrepreneur.

4. Turn "impossible" into "possible." The moment you actually believe that your business goals can be met is when they begin to happen.

5. Use what you have to get started. Don't avoid your entrepreneurial goals because you don't have an ideal situation. Lack of start-up money is completely normal, and lack of support from family and friends is typical. The first step may be the hardest, but without it there's no second step.

6. Be realistic. If you think you're going to build a successful company overnight, you're setting yourself up for failure. If you think you're going to do it in a year, you're again setting yourself up for a big letdown. Be realistic. Most goals take time to achieve.

7. Live by the law of productivity. This law is simple. Get things done. If you've been working all day (or all week), and have nothing to show for it, you're not a productive worker.

8. It's never too late. People 50 years of age and older are more likely than younger folks to own their own businesses. It's never too late to be an entrepreneur.

9. Incorporate early. It is generally in your best interest to incorporate as soon as possible for reasons that go far beyond tax savings. Being incorporated fully protects you as an individual from any lawsuits, and may enhance your image and prestige in the eyes of clients or suppliers.

10. Home-based businesses work. Most customers do not care if you are working out of your home. Maintaining an expensive office space can lead to escalating debt and business failure. What matters most to clients is whether they are getting cost-effective results or not.

THE ENTREPRENEURIAL MIND-SET

CHAPTER 9

OPTIMISTS LIVE LONGER THAN PESSIMISTS

Chances are that 2009 was not a very good business year for you. It's possible yours was among the thousands of companies that folded, or the millions that downsized to cut expenses.

Despite this, you have every reason to be optimistic about the future. Why? Because life is full of peaks and valleys. When you're in a valley, there's a peak just ahead. If you believe that things will improve, they will—as long as you continue to work hard to make it happen.

The reason why optimistic people live longer than pessimistic people is because optimistic people keep themselves alive. When faced with a challenge, they not only think positively but also act in harmony with that challenge. Instead of giving up, they keep at it—and eventually begin to see progress, which in turn motivates them to press on.

Pessimistic people, on the contrary, worry themselves into the grave. Their negative energy and lack of hope buries them fast. They develop health problems, low self-esteem, and before you know it they've lost all motivation. Recovery never happens because there is no environment to support it.

No matter what happened this year, next year is a fresh start. 2009 was the year of the whine, but 2010 is the year of the grin.

So pick up your swagger and make it happen.

• ▣ • ▣ • ▣ •

Do You Have the Nerve to Be Courageous?

It's good to have a healthy fear of failing in business—it will keep you from making unwise decisions. However, don't allow fear to inhibit your ideas. In other words, don't allow the fear of failing to be the reason you never gave it a shot.

Here is the dictionary definition of the word *entrepreneur*: a person who *takes the risk* of organizing and operating a new business venture.

Yes, business is a risk. If you call yourself an entrepreneur, then you are a risk-taker. You cannot be an entrepreneur if you do not courageously step outside your comfort boundaries to pursue a business idea.

Successful businessmen and women are courageous. They understand that business is risky, and are willing to move forward despite this. Potentially losing money doesn't hold them back from pursuing their goals.

You must understand that every business will assume risk of some sort, and will suffer sometimes because of it. This may very well mean losing money. But also understand that risk has led to tons of success stories.

Grasp what I'm saying here, and your success story could be next. Fully understand what it means to wear the mantle of "entrepreneur."

● ▣ ● ▣ ● ▣ ●

Being Positive Is Good, But It's Not Enough

It's good to be a positive thinker, but don't think for one second that that's all you have to do. Being a successful entrepreneur requires more than just having an optimistic outlook.

Some people believe that they should spend all their time listening to motivational speakers, staying inspired—and the rest will happen. This is false reasoning.

I don't care how motivated you are, you will not be successful until you become a hard worker. Hard work means putting in the time and energy that it takes to build a company. Some people say, "Don't work hard, work smart." Truth be told, you need to work hard *and* smart because building a profitable business requires genuine effort.

Don't be mistaken. I'm not trying to downplay being optimistic. I just think a lot of people are confused. They superstitiously believe that success is guaranteed to those who are "strong believers." This has been referred to as "The Law of Attraction."

The only law I'm familiar with in business is the "The Law of Productivity." It's about getting things accomplished, and closing out each day with several tasks completed.

Ask any successful entrepreneur, and they'll tell you that thinking positive is only a small factor of the equation. You have to get your hands dirty and get some work done. Understand that there are no shortcuts in business. You *cannot* take the elevator to success, you have to take the stairs—and these stairs are steep with no handrails.

So think positively, but also think realistically. Success is not just itching to come your way. You have to go get it!

• ▣ • ▣ • ▣ •

LEARN TO HAVE THICK SKIN

Any successful person will tell you that you need "thick skin" (like that of an elephant) to survive in business. Having thick skin means you have the ability to withstand criticism, handle confrontation, and put your foot down when you have to.

This means that, as an employer, you have to be able to fire people when necessary, and turn down unwarranted requests for raises. There is no room for emotional attachments or relationships in the workplace. This is exactly why many people don't recommend hiring family members.

Business can be very cutthroat. Your clients will come down on you in a heartbeat if they aren't happy with your service or product. Your creditors will come down on you if they aren't paid on time. So you have to come down on your staff when their performance is unsatisfactory.

You don't have to be mean or rude, just tough.

• ▣ • ▣ • ▣ •

BE PROGRESSIVE

Take a long hard look at your business. Are you in the same place you were last year? If so, you haven't made any progress and have just wasted precious time that you'll never get back.

Being progressive means to take small consistent steps that add up to big ones. It means that you are slowly (but surely) making your way to success.

You may be losing money on your business, but if you're losing less and less each month you'll eventually break even, and then hit profitability. You may not have as many clients as you'd like, but if you keep offering that unforgettable customer service, word will get around.

Tom Joyner and Oprah may not have called you back to be on their shows, but if you're doing interviews on smaller radio shows you'll eventually become the go-to person for your industry. Your book may not be on the bestseller list, but if you keep pushing it at small functions you'll create a demand that bookstores and readers won't be able to ignore.

Remember this always: Time will go on with or without you. Moving forward slowly is better than not moving at all. So, be progressive and don't give up.

• ▣ • ▣ • ▣ •

ARE YOU YOUR WORST ENEMY?

There are many factors that can contribute to a business failing: lack of advertising, poor management of staff, bad customer service, tax trouble, etc. However, many entrepreneurs don't realize that sometimes the problem is the one thing you never think of: you.

That's right, it could very well be true that *you* are your company's worst enemy.

Perhaps your personality is too aggressive and you turn potential clients away. Maybe your personality is too soft and you aren't convincing enough to potential clients.

Could it be that you're too lazy and lack a strong work ethic? Or you work too hard and are always too tired to pay attention to new opportunities?

Maybe you're too stubborn. Or ignorant and slow to adapt. Perhaps you change too quickly and people can't keep up with you.

Do you blame others instead of taking responsibility when things go wrong? As a result of your denial, perhaps you repeat the same mistakes over and over again.

Conduct an honest self-analysis. Determine to find your own blind spots. Ask others what they think about you as a business owner, and how you run your company. Listen closely to what they say, and take action.

• ▣ • ▣ • ▣ •

IS YOUR MIND FIXED?

Is it your goal to one day own a five-star hotel in downtown San Francisco on the water with a view of the Bay Bridge? Are you so stuck on that concept that you reject other viable business opportunities that practically fall into your lap?

What would you do if the opportunity came along for you to own a three-star hotel in a small town in Arkansas? Or a three-star hotel in the Mojave Desert? Or even a hotel in the blustery cold of Minnesota? Would you turn these down just because they don't fit what you originally had in mind?

Many entrepreneurs would, in fact, turn down these opportunities because their minds are fixed on a business plan with very detailed specifics. "It has to be San Francisco," they might say. "And it has to be downtown by the water." However, like most people who have their minds fixed with all their eggs in one basket—they will likely end up with nothing.

Never forfeit a prime opportunity that fits your aspirations just because you have something else in mind. Reaching your business goals is about making sacrifices and building stepping stones. This may require you having to live in a less desirable area, and even pursuing a less desirable course.

Be realistic and learn quickly that your big goals will take time to attain, and you'll get there by setting smaller, reachable goals. Attempting to skip to the end will only leave you with nothing at all.

Remember how we all had to take classes that we didn't like in high school? But after only a short investment of time and energy, it all led up to the big graduation day. Imagine trying to graduate high school without having attended any classes. You will not be successful.

Business is no different. You have to "pay your dues" by making sacrifices. True entrepreneurs recognize this early on, and will be happy to do so. They know that, in time, they'll reach their long-term goals. Until then, they also know that their passion for business will keep them motivated.

• ▣ • ▣ • ▣ •

STOP DRAGGING YOUR FEET

Have you been working on your website for six months and it still hasn't gone live? Have you been writing your business plan for a year, and your business still hasn't launched? If this sounds like you, you're dragging your feet.

Building a website or writing a business plan (like many other steps to starting a business) shouldn't take you longer than one or two weeks. If it's taking longer, you're moving too slowly.

You need to hurry up and get these items out of the way, so you can move on to the bigger and better things. The clock is ticking and you're losing time that you'll never get back.

There's no need to rush when starting a business because there's no race. However, you do need to have a sense of urgency. In other words, learn to keep it moving.

Building a successful business is already a long process. Don't make it any longer than it has to be.

Imagine going to college to earn a four-year degree, and taking only one class every year (not per semester—per year). You just turned a four-year small project into a 12- to 15-year massive endeavor.

Moral of the story: Don't drag your feet!

• ▣ • ▣ • ▣ •

If It Doesn't Make Sense, Don't Do It

For some strange reason, it's very common for people to make business or life decisions that even they know don't make sense. In many cases, the reason is intimidation, pressure, being thoughtless, or just plain gullible.

People resort to doing things that don't make sense when they feel they have no other options. Well, you do have an option: the option to not do it.

Here are some tips to avoid making unwise business decisions:

1. *Don't fall for the sales pitch.* Don't allow sales people to pressure you into buying something your company doesn't need. Be abrupt. Hurt their feelings if you have to.

2. *Don't be gullible.* Stop believing everything people tell you. Question everything—especially business advice. So what if he's a lawyer or an MBA or a PhD? Lawyers, doctors, and other professionals give bad advice every single day. Double-check what people are telling you.

3. *Be realistic.* Does it sound realistic that you can get two million e-mail addresses for only 100 bucks? If it sounds far-fetched it almost certainly is.

4. *Stay focused.* Don't take your eye off the bottom line. If you're getting ready to make a business decision that's not going to help your bottom line, then it's probably not a good decision.

• ▣ • ▣ • ▣ •

Don't Allow Your Personal Issues to Destroy Your Business

Whatever is going wrong in your personal life (marital issues, problems with kids, sickness or death in the family, etc.), you must keep it away from your business affairs.

If not, your company will be adversely affected, which will begin to be apparent in many different ways. Your productivity will slow down, your creativity will diminish, and your profits will drop. Even worse, you will be unmotivated to do anything about it.

Consider this experience from Linda Finkle, an expert on organizational communication:

"Many years ago I was dealing with an issue that involved one of my children. It was a difficult and very challenging time for me and the rest of my family. A few close friends knew, but I felt that I couldn't or shouldn't let others know. . .Then one day, a client told me she thought I wasn't interested in her as a client anymore. When I asked why, she confided that I seemed distracted when we met and that I didn't send her e-mails or respond to her as I had in the past. I realized that while I thought I had myself under control, I didn't."

Finkle advises, "During difficult times, size up your work load and priorities. Focus on what must be done and let everything else go. Make a point of reminding yourself that you can't do it all, and only the things that absolutely must be done will get attention."

She continues, "Ask for help from others and accept it graciously. For some reason, most people are hesitant or embarrassed about asking for help. It is during these times that we need others the most, so don't deprive yourself during these difficult times. And remember to take time for yourself. Going through a trying time will wear on you emotionally and physically, so take time to go to the gym, play golf, read a book or take a long, relaxing bath."

In addition to this, my advice is to learn to compartmentalize—separate your mind into isolated segments or categories. This way, the personal issues you're facing will only have an impact on your personal life—and vice versa.

We all have problems and we all face difficulty from time to time. That's life. However, a successful entrepreneur knows how to simultaneously weather the storm and keep his/her business both afloat and profitable. This is easier said than done, but it can be accomplished.

• ▣ • ▣ • ▣ •

THE FAMILY'S BUSINESS VS. YOUR BUSINESS

On more than one occasion, I've seen family members come together to financially contribute to a wedding: $3,000 for flowers, $1,000 for a chocolate fountain, $5,000 for a wedding dress. No exaggeration: I've seen low-income families come together and raise thousands of dollars for a wedding that lasted a few hours, and a marriage that lasted a few years.

This same energy and passion should be used to come together to invest in a business that can make everyone wealthy, can last a lifetime, and can be passed down to future generations.

If a family got together and raised just a couple thousand dollars, they can open a store front, buy a franchise, or even expand an existing business.

Why not organize your family to invest in something that will yield a return and produce results that can financially empower everyone?

• ▣ • ▣ • ▣ •

ARE YOU PLACING TOO MUCH
EMPHASIS ON THE WRONG THINGS?

Your glossy colorful business cards are ready, and your new logo is looking fresh-to-def. You're wearing the right colors, your shoes are polished, and you're planning to do some really firm handshakes looking people right in the eye. Your shoes match your belt, and your belt matches your handbag or briefcase. You've even got your underwear matching your socks. You're wearing your new Rolex and an Armani suit, so that people can think you're rolling in dough.

You attend your conference or business meeting or networking function, and you do everything just as you practiced. But at the end of the day, you get little to no results. What happened? You did everything right, didn't you?

Well, if you're like many people, you may have put too much emphasis on all the wrong things.

There's nothing wrong with glossy business cards and a colorful logo, but that's not what's going to sell your product or service. Looking nice and wearing "business" colors is a plus, but this too will not seal the deal.

What sells your products and services is—your products and services. What you have to offer should sell itself. That's where the emphasis needs to be placed—there and also on your sales presentation. At the end of the day, people don't care about anything other than whether or not they need or want what you're selling.

Think about it: When was the last time you bought something because you liked how firm the salesperson shook your hand? Or because you liked their logo? Or because you were impressed with the way that person dressed?

You, like many other consumers, buy for one reason: Because you're impressed and are convinced that this product or service should be a part of your life. Whether you were sold through a sales presentation (one-on-one consultation, brochure, radio/TV ad, website, etc.) or whether the product sold itself—the emphasis was placed heavily on what was being sold.

Professionalism is extremely important in many ways, but if you don't have a product or service that people want, you can forget it.

• ▣ • ▣ • ▣ •

NOT EVERY "GOOD IDEA" IS A GOOD IDEA

Coming up with a good business idea doesn't necessarily mean that you should pursue it. This may sound unorthodox, but many good ideas should be left alone. A "good idea" can cost you a lot of money, a lot of time, and bring you no results.

Here are some questions to ask yourself before you pursue a "good idea":

1. *Is this idea easily duplicable?*
   Trademarks and patents can protect your idea, but not every idea can be trademarked or patented. For instance, if you have a unique service to provide, you may not necessarily own it exclusively. If a bigger company with more resources notices that you're on to something, they might easily (and legally) steal your idea and create a major challenge for you.

2. *Does this idea require a lot of funding?*
   Many entrepreneurs have great ideas, but fail to realize that some are just too expensive. Bringing in investors and venture capitalists to solve this problem can be a complicated process, and you'll be giving up ownership shares. I would never discourage an entrepreneur from seeking funding, but make sure you know what you're doing.

3. *Do I have the expertise to bring this idea to life?*
   You may have a good idea about the end product, but make sure that you fully understand and have experience in the field to get the job done. Be realistic.

If you have a very innovative technological idea, you must also have the knowledge and intuition to bring it to fruition. This may mean hiring those whose expertise complements what you don't know. Otherwise, your idea will always be just an idea.

4. *Will the patent for this idea expire before it comes to life?* Many entrepreneurs tend to forget that a federal patent expires in 10 years. Unfortunately, it can take that long to make your idea come alive. If your idea has not become successful within that period, your patent will expire and your idea becomes open and available for anyone to use.

· ▣ · ▣ · ▣ ·

ALMOST DOESN'T COUNT

Either you're going to see this thing through, or you're not. There are no in-betweens. If you quit and never make it, you haven't earned the right to call yourself an entrepreneur. Think of it this way: Does a high school student who drops out before graduation get credit for attending grades 9, 10, and 11? Do people talk for long about the candidate who was running for office and lost by one vote? Do basketball fans remember the point guard who almost made the last-minute shot? Do football fans remember the wide receiver who almost caught the touchdown pass with no time left on the clock?

In all of these scenarios, the individual *almost* made it. However, the reality is that "almost" doesn't count. Likewise, you can spend as much money and time as you want on starting a business—but if you quit before you reach success, it doesn't count. People don't walk around saying, "I almost was a successful entrepreneur" because they know that no one wants to hear that.

Always remember that it's okay to give up on a business idea, but never give up in business.

• ▣ • ▣ • ▣ •

Four Things an Entrepreneur Should Never Say

Nearly every time I'm networking at a business function, I run into people who say things that make me question whether or not they're legit. Here are just some that I've heard:

- *Our website gets millions of hits.* First of all, web traffic is not measured in "hits" anymore; it's measured in impressions, page views, and unique visitors. Secondly, your website doesn't get millions of hits. If it did, people would already know and you wouldn't have to broadcast it. Thirdly, I went to your website before and the design stinks. There's no way a million people go there.

- *We real big right now.* First of all, the proper way to say that is "We're really big right now." Second, no you're not. If you were "real big" I'd already know and so would everybody else. Third, what does that mean? Your statement doesn't mean anything. How are you big? Why are you big? Big in sales? Big in popularity?

- *I'm the hottest thing out.* You're hot? Do you mean you're getting tons of publicity? Do you mean you're in high demand? What newspapers have you been featured in? Any radio and TV shows? Generally, people who are the "hottest thing out" don't have to tell people that because people already know.

- *I own my own business in network marketing.* You might be making some money, but if you're in network marketing, you don't own anything. You work for somebody else. You're a contractor who gets paid on commission. Just tell people you "work in network marketing."

• ▣ • ▣ • ▣ •

DO WHAT EVERYBODY ELSE IS NOT DOING

In normal economic conditions, it's always in your best interest to outthink your competition. During a recession, it's even more important. The key is to try to do things that no one else is doing or even thinking of.

Many entrepreneurs like to take the easy, less demanding route. But now is the time to welcome the difficult tasks. These will take forever to complete but will pay off greatly.

You know what they are. You've been avoiding them for quite some time. Start chipping away today. A thousand-mile journey begins with the first step. Also, now is the time to be bold and take risks. I'm not advising you to be careless, but I'm encouraging you to live up to your entrepreneurial title.

A recession can create lots of opportunities for you that aren't normally available. For instance, many companies struggle during a recession—which can create an opportunity for you to buy your competitor out. In addition, many companies will cut their advertising budgets—which can create an opportunity for you to increase your budget and take over their market share.

These are general tips, but take a good look at your business model. Pursue a course that your competition hasn't thought of.

• ▣ • ▣ • ▣ •

OVERCOME THE FOUR BARRIERS OF CHANGE

There may be several things that are holding you back from reaching your business goals. More than likely, change is one of them. Speaker and author John Baker founder of READY Thinking, LLC asserts that change is the miracle that stimulates growth. Without it, your business does not grow.

Baker identified the following four barriers to change:

- Fear

- The "what if" game

- Labels and titles (for example, losing your VP title in corporate America)

- Lack of focus

Fear is undoubtedly the most popular one, although it shouldn't be. If you want to truly call yourself an entrepreneur, you must be able and willing to take risks. Risk takers are not afraid of failure. In fact, they expect it to happen from time to time. This is a good thing.

Think of a baby learning to walk. Doing so is risky because it may fall and get hurt—and that happens. However, this doesn't stop the baby from learning to walk. That's because babies instinctively realize that it's time for change. It's time to stop crawling and start walking. It's time for growth.

Likewise, it's time for a change in you. Whether you're just starting out in business, or have been a business owner for years—it's time to elevate your game.

Take some new steps. You'll fall, but you'll learn from that fall and will be humbled. After a few falls, you'll learn how to take the right steps with the right balance. Then the growth factor will kick in and advance you to the next level.

● ▣ ● ▣ ● ▣ ●

HOW TO FAIL IN BUSINESS

The U.S. Census Bureau states that African Americans are more likely to *start* a business than their white counterparts. That same report reveals that African Americans are also more likely to *fail* in business within the first five years.

If you're interested in joining the thousands of other black-owned firms that flop every single year (I'm being ironic), pay very close attention.

Here's what happens step by step:

1. A wealth-conscious African American decides that he wants a better life for himself and his family.

2. He decides to start a small business, or join a network marketing company.

3. Because he's so excited and zealous (either from self-motivation or from listening to motivational speakers), he focuses on *what* he is selling instead of *how* to sell it and *whom* to sell it to.

4. Most time and energy is spent on preparation (website development, business cards, letterhead, etc.), but little to no time on realistically planning the marketing strategy and demographically assessing the target market.

5. Months will go by. Little (if any) revenue has been generated. He decides to give it one last try, invest more money and randomly pick an advertising method, such as taking out a newspaper ad or passing out flyers. This, again, generates little revenue.

6. Tired and frustrated, he decides to give up on pursuing a better life and join the masses of black entrepreneurs who never made it.

The Major Pitfall: There was never a realistic marketing plan that made sense.

The Solution: Business is 10 percent what you're selling, and 90 percent who you're selling it to. Do not spend most of your time and energy on the product. Spend it on the marketing campaign.

It doesn't matter what you're selling. If you don't know how to market to potential buyers (more than just family and friends), you really aren't selling anything.

• ▣ • ▣ • ▣ •

DON'T OVERSIMPLIFY BUSINESS

Business *is* simple in a way, but don't oversimplify it. Whether you're planning to launch a company or already running one, always remember that it takes hard work and smart thinking to stay afloat.

Often I hear people say, "All you have to do is...", but this is the wrong way to start a sentence when discussing how to build or manage a company. It's not about one or two steps, or some type of overnight solution. It's about patience and long-term diligence. It's about strategizing and blueprinting, and properly managing your resources.

Business is simple only in the sense that it can be defined in one statement: the exchange of currency for products and services.

Business involves many components. There's advertising, public relations, sales, logistics, accounting, management, human resources, law, and more. Staying on top of all of these doesn't always ensure profitability.

Don't be mistaken: Simplicity does not mean that it's super-easy.

• ▣ • ▣ • ▣ •

LEARN, NOT "BURN," FROM YOUR MISTAKES

We all have made bad business decisions. Some of them were quite dumb, others were just from bad instinct. Maybe you lost money, wasted time, or even both. Despite this, you must recognize that making business mistakes is a natural part of building your career as an entrepreneur.

Here's the key: When you do make a business mistake, learn from it. Start by fully accepting the blame and responsibility, and not putting it on others. There are very few cases when you can place the blame on someone else other than yourself, and this is very easy to determine.

All you have to do is ask yourself, "Was there something I could have done to prevent this?" If the answer is yes, then it was your fault. If the answer is no (which it rarely is), then it wasn't your fault.

The point is that the minute you accept full responsibility, that's the moment you actually learn something valuable from your mistakes. As a mature adult, your brain is automatically trained to not make the same unwise decisions over and over again. However, your brain is waiting for you to admit that it was you who actually made the mistake.

Some people, however, end up "burning" from their mistakes. Instead of admitting that they were at fault, they blame other people or other factors. They say things like "He screwed me over," instead of, "Maybe I should have looked closer at the contract." They say things like "He stole my idea" instead of "I should have better protected my idea through patents and trademarks." Or even "He didn't do what he said he'd do," instead of, "I should have gotten that in writing."

They "burn" from their mistakes because in the future, when they face a similar scenario, they'll make the same mistake again... and again and again. Why? Because their brain is telling them that last time it wasn't their fault, so there's no reason to proceed cautiously this time.

The only way to grow in business is to learn, not "burn" from your errors. We all make bad decisions, but how you respond determines how successful you'll be.

• ▣ • ▣ • ▣ •

YOU DON'T HAVE TO BE A PILOT TO START AN AIRLINE

You may respond to this by saying, "I'm not interested in starting an airline." Well, neither am I. The point is to emphasize that you don't have to possess industry skills to start a company in a particular industry.

In other words, if you want to start an airline you don't need to learn how to fly. If you want to start a software company, you don't have to be a programmer. If you want to start a catering company, you don't have to be a chef. The only thing you need to know in these instances is how to find and manage a pilot, a programmer, and a chef. And of course, it would be good to at least understand how these different industries work.

Too often though, entrepreneurs will come up with a great idea for a business but dismiss that idea after they realize that they don't have the needed skills. Well, with the exception of certain cases, like Bill Gates who was a programmer who started a software company, most scenarios are quite the opposite.

For instance, Collett E. Woolman, founder of Delta Airlines, was not a pilot. Also, Pierre Bellon, founder of Sodexho (a large catering and food services company), is not a cook and has never been one.

Broaden your sense of thinking when it comes to business. While you should pursue business endeavors that interest you, don't just stick to ideas that encompass your skill level.

Running a successful business is about management and marketing. Manage the people who have the skills, market those skills to potential customers, and go down in history as a successful businessperson.

● ▣ ● ▣ ● ▣ ●

THE FORMULA: WHY TYLER PERRY WILL ALWAYS BE IN BUSINESS

In just a few years, filmmaker Tyler Perry has gone from producing local plays to producing a television series, a talk show and now internationally distributed films. Everything he has done so far has worked. What's his secret? Does he have good luck?

There are no secrets, and luck is a minor player. Put simply: Tyler Perry has a formula, and has stuck to it in everything he does. Just like in science, a particular formula yields a particular result. If there's one drop too much or too little, there will be a different outcome.

Formulas in business don't work much differently from formulas in science. When you find something that yields a particular result, desired or undesired, you either stick with it, or swiftly depart from it. Perry has found a formula that works.

His formula (comedy + family values + morals = revenue) has yielded him years and years of success, with millions of fans worldwide.

What's the formula for your company? Do you even have a formula? Finding the right formula for your company can yield positive financial results. Know your audience. Know who it is that will utilize your product or service, and find out what they want and how they want it. Once you discover that need, you fill it—and keep filling it.

The process of filling the need can be done in various ways. Find out the best ways and exploit them in every permutation possible. Be creative and innovative. Reinvent the wheel if you have to. The right formula will transform your business into an invaluable product or service that your customers cannot do without.

Yes, under the right conditions liquid can turn into a solid and a solid can become a liquid. So find what works and don't ever lose sight of what got you in business and what keeps you in business. Tyler Perry knows this and lives this wisdom well. Although he may choose to innovate, Perry never deviates from the fundamental winning formula that established his core business.

• ▣ • ▣ • ▣ •

AIM HIGH, BUT NOT TOO HIGH

If you think you're going to build a successful company overnight, you're setting yourself up for a big letdown. If you think you're going to do it in a year, you're again setting yourself up for a big letdown. Think realistically. Most goals take time to achieve.

Why not make a five-year plan outlining small goals that will lead to your big goals? Five years is not a long time at all, and is a very realistic time frame to achieve what you want.

Many folks are okay with the idea of taking four years to earn a high school diploma, and another four years to earn a college degree. But many feel that four to five years to build a company is just too long to wait. The point is to aim high, but be reasonable about how high you're aiming. It wouldn't make much sense for a high school-bound student to have the goal of earning a diploma in one year. It's a four-year process.

Likewise, building a company is a process. You should set high standards and challenge yourself to do what may seem unthinkable. However, setting goals that are too high or unachievable will only discourage you.

When you want to accomplish something, don't ignore the odds that you're up against. Rather, consider them and realize that you *can* beat these odds if they're within reasonable bounds—keeping in mind that you're not superhuman.

Building a successful business is a process that requires a lot of time and energy. How high you're aiming should be based on a realistic timeline.

Remember, doing too much at once can backfire. And believe it or not, growing too fast can be a bad thing.

● ▣ ● ▣ ● ▣ ●

"IT MUST NOT HURT THAT BAD"

My mom once told me a story about a dog that sat on the porch howling in pain all day and all night. People in the neighborhood would always hear the dog and wonder why he was constantly howling. One day a neighbor was walking by the house, and the owner was on the porch with the dog.

"Why does your dog howl like that? He sounds like he's in pain," the neighbor said.

"He is in pain," said the owner. "He's sitting on a nail."

"A nail," the neighbor said. "Is he stuck?"

"Nope," said the owner.

"So why doesn't he just get up?" asked the neighbor.

The owner replied: "It must not hurt that bad."

The moral of the story: many people complain extensively about their situations, but do little or nothing to try and change things. Unfortunately, onlookers have to conclude that it really must not be that bad. Surely you know someone like this. But ask yourself—"Am I like this?"

Many complain about their financial status, but then make excuses about the solution that's right in front of their face. Here's an example:

A friend from the Washington, D.C. area once told me that he was struggling really hard to make ends meet. He said he had a goal to start a business but simply couldn't afford to do so. I asked him if there was anything keeping him tied to the D.C. area. He said no.

So, I encouraged him to move south to Virginia or North Carolina. Both states have lower costs of living and he would pay half what he's paying to live in D.C. In addition, he could start a business with lower start-up funds and a less saturated market.

His response was: "Ain't nothing to do down there." My response was: "It must not hurt that bad."

Change the direction of your life starting today. Stop suffering from self-inflicted wounds. If you can do something about your situation, then do it. Stop making excuses, stop procrastinating, and do it!

• ▣ • ▣ • ▣ •

YOU CAN READ, BUT CAN YOU WRITE?

It surprises me that many entrepreneurs and business owners have poor writing skills. This is often displayed when they write e-mails, press releases, columns, blogs, books, and more.

Critical mistakes I've seen include improper use of single and double quotes, improper use or lack of commas, and even a lack of periods. I've also seen well-known, reputable individuals write long e-mails that are not properly divided into paragraphs, and contain incomplete sentences.

I don't consider myself to be a writing expert, but I've learned how to write effectively because I know it can affect my company's revenue.

For instance, I deal with a lot of key executives at major corporations. Can you imagine how they'd feel if I sent them an e-mail with misspelled words? In just a moment's time, they may lose confidence in me and my company.

I also blog regularly and send out press releases regarding my company, with the goal of encouraging more clients to do business with us. Can you imagine how people would feel if the content was poorly written with incomplete thoughts? Again, in just a moment's time, they can be discouraged about reaching out to me.

Always remember that how you write will determine what people think of you. You can be a great businessperson and even a great speaker, but if your writing skills are weak, it can harm your reputation.

You don't have to be a perfectionist and write as if you're being monitored by the grammar police, but you should master basic writing skills. If necessary, use your Spell Check and ALWAYS get several people to proofread your final work.

• ▣ • ▣ • ▣ •

A JACK OR JILL OF ALL TRADES—GOOD OR BAD?

Contrary to popular belief, it's perfectly okay to be a Jack of All Trades. This phrase is commonly used to describe an entrepreneur or business owner that possesses many skills and offers many different services to customers.

If this describes you, that's good. Many well-known entrepreneurs, such as Oprah Winfrey, Donald Trump, Ted Turner, Warren Buffett, etc., have several different companies that offer a variety of services. They understand that it's smart to have multiple streams of income in case one suffers a downturn.

Even rap artists have found great success with this approach. They own rap labels, film companies, clothing companies, shoe companies, jewelry companies, and often local restaurants in their hometowns.

While it's perfectly okay to be a Jack of All Trades, don't make the fatal mistake of combining all your services into one company. For instance, it's a terrible idea to indicate on your business card or website that you're a lawn doctor, web developer, photographer, and interior designer.

Instead, create a different company (and website) for each unique service that you provide so potential customers won't be inundated with services and products they have no interest in. Instead, they'll only see information pertaining to what they're inquiring about.

Also, they'll perceive you as a highly skilled professional who knows what you're doing. If they see too many different services offered, they may assume that you're not an expert at anything but just have a lot of superficial knowledge. That, of course, is not the impression you want to give.

• ▣ • ▣ • ▣ •

BIGGER IS NOT ALWAYS BETTER

Many believe that a company's level of success is based entirely on its size. This is not always true. Having more employees and large office space doesn't necessarily give you an advantage.

A small company with just one or two employees and no office space can easily be more profitable and can compete with, and often outmaneuver, a bigger company. Even more, a small company can be more simple and less stressful to manage than a large one.

In the age of the dot com, it's very common for successful businesses to be run by one or two people who work at home. These types of businesses can typically generate anywhere from $30,000 to $1,000,000+ a year.

Circumstances are very different from 10 or 20 years ago—you don't need a storefront to build a business and you don't necessarily need office space. It can all be done virtually.

I know some Americans who live overseas and run their businesses online—with all of their customers in the United States. Not only do they not have to deal with their customers face-to-face, but they don't even have to be on the same continent.

So as you formulate or reformulate your business ideas, think big—but also think small. Keep your overhead low. Being able to afford office space doesn't mean you must have it. The same goes for multiple employees. Determine how to run your business in the most simple, cost-effective way possible, and whenever possible, keep the size of your company to a minimum.

• ▣ • ▣ • ▣ •

BLAME YOURSELF

To move forward in business, sometimes YOU have to accept the blame. The moment you realize this, your company will flourish. Entrepreneurs who don't admit to their mistakes will likely make the same mistakes over and over again.

I've seen many musicians blame their record labels for lack of promotion when their CDs don't sell. However, most of the time it's their music that just wasn't good enough.

I've seen tons of black entrepreneurs blame their lack of success on "the industry," "the timing," or "the location." Some people will even blame the targeted consumers who didn't buy into their ideas. "People are stupid for not seeing the benefit of what I'm selling," they say.

When things go wrong in business, you have to realistically assess what happened. If all fingers point at you, then accept the blame and learn from your mistakes.

Every business owner will make bad decisions and take a loss. This is a completely normal and necessary learning process. Accept it, absorb the damage, and move on.

• ▣ • ▣ • ▣ •

THE LIGHT AT THE END OF THE TUNNEL

Sometimes you may feel that you're in a dark tunnel and the bright light at the end is an oncoming train. But you're mistaken. That light at the end of the tunnel is the way out getting closer and closer!

Building a business is hard, and many times it may seem like you're doomed. The key is to be optimistic. Hard work always pays off, and you'll soon reap the rewards. You just have to keep at it.

Remember that Donald Trump once found himself in billions of dollars of debt, but he found a way to rebound and is now known as the Real Estate King.

Remember that Bill Gates once found himself struggling to convince people that his Windows operating system was a billion-dollar concept. Now, he's a billionaire 80 times over.

Remember how difficult it was for Bob Johnson to launch BET—the first-ever nationally syndicated black channel. Today BET is a three-billion-dollar empire.

These types of success stories are not uncommon, and your story is next. So get back to the basics and figure out what you need to do to remedy or enhance your situation. Once you determine what your personal success recipe is, stick to it and don't deviate.

● ▣ ● ▣ ● ▣ ●

DOES MONEY EQUAL POWER?

This question can be argued by many different people from many different angles, and each time you'd get a different answer. My answer would be "no." I don't believe that money gives you power. Having a lot of money just gives you freedom. Freedom from working, and freedom to go wherever you want to go and do whatever you want to do.

Power is different. Power is when you're influential. People follow you. People respect you. People listen to what you have to say and take action.

As an entrepreneur, don't focus so much on making a lot of money. The money will come in due course. Rather, focus on being powerful and influential. Make people view you as a resource they can't do without. Motivate them to follow you on Twitter and subscribe to your blog. Reinforce their belief that they should read all your books, and participate in your teleseminars and webinars.

Over time, your followers will become your clients, and your clients will refer you to more followers. Before you know it, you're considered an expert or a guru or even a mogul.

Consider Martin Luther King, Jr. He was not a rich man, but he was a very powerful man. Can you imagine how many books he would have sold if he were still alive today? Can you imagine how many people would attend his conferences? Can you imagine how many subscribers he would have to his blog?

That, my friend, is the power of power.

BE A "NO" MAN

It is a common misconception that to be in business you have to say "yes" to everything that is proposed to you. This is not true. A good business person knows how to say "no."

When you must say no, tell your customer why and then offer alternatives. If you can't meet a requested deadline, be honest about your capabilities, offer the customer a deadline you can meet and, if that's not acceptable, provide a referral to another source. Otherwise, being a yes man will have you involved in all kinds of activities that are not helping your business.

Saying no can be a big part of your overall success strategy. In the long run people will respect your honesty. And who knows? You may actually find that people will begin to approach you with the right ideas that will help you achieve success on your terms.

CHAPTER 10

BEST PRACTICES

THE PROS AND CONS OF FIVE-DAY USPS MAIL DELIVERY

The number of items handled by the United States Postal Service each year is decreasing by the billions. It's estimated that, by the year 2020, the amount will be reduced by up to 55 percent. Therefore, the USPS needs to cut costs immediately or the organization will become victim to a huge financial disaster.

To save $3.3 billion annually, the United States Postal Service is proposing to switch to a five-day mail delivery week. If enforced, mail will no longer be delivered on Saturdays starting in 2011.

Here are the potential pros for entrepreneurs:

- *Reduced and/or more stable direct mail costs*
  Direct mail advertising via postcards, catalogs, and sales letters is extremely effective for many businesses. However, the cost to mail out these items increases nearly every year because of the USPS's financial problems. If it is able to cut costs by enforcing five-day mail delivery, the price of bulk postage could go down. If not, perhaps it won't increase as often.

- *An extra day to pay invoices*
  Like most entrepreneurs in this economy, many businesses are struggling to stay afloat. Mail not

being delivered on Saturday gives them an extra day to pay an outstanding invoice or a bill. One day isn't much, but may occasionally be just enough to get the cash flow needed.

Here are the potential cons for entrepreneurs:

- *Late payments from your clients*
  Just like you have an extra day t*o pay your bills, so too will* your clients. If you don't receive a much needed check by Friday, now you have to wait until Monday. This can causes problems if your office rent or other expenses are due over the weekend.

- *Less time to organize mail*
  Credit card companies and other organizations receive thousands of pieces of mail a day, and have hired a Saturday staff to retrieve and process it. If Saturday mail is done away with, this means that these types of companies will only have five days a week to get the job done.

- *More airfare*
  You may or may not be aware of this, but the USPS does not have its own airplanes, like UPS and FedEx, to transport mail. They use the same airlines you fly on—Southwest, United, Delta, etc.

If mail delivery is reduced to a five-day week, many people may stop using the USPS and start using another mailing service, or just e-mail and fax. If this happens, it could drastically reduce the revenue paid to the airlines by the USPS. The airlines, in turn, may increase airfares to make up the difference.

• ▣ • ▣ • ▣ •

Using a Free E-mail Address Is Bad for Business

If you're a company, an organization, or just an individual brand, you should not be using free e-mail address accounts as your primary form of communication.

What's a free e-mail account? Any e-mail address that ends in @hotmail.com, @yahoo.com, @gmail.com, @aol.com, etc. If your name is Grace and the name of your business is Grace Publishing, it makes you look unprofessional and "small" if your primary e-mail address is gracepublishing@yahoo.com. Instead, your primary e-mail address should be grace@gracepublishing.com or even info@gracepublishing.com hosted on your own domain name.

This simple implementation will make your company (and you) sound and look a lot more legit. Even more, it looks better on your business cards and on your promo material.

Setting up and managing email addresses on your own domain is very easy to do. It's called business email hosting. There are several affordable services that can help you with this. I recommend Everyone.net, Gmail Business, or RackSpace.com. Of the three, I like Gmail Business the best because it only charges you $50 a year per address, and its functionality is very impressive. Making the change will only take a few minutes and the configuration will be complete in just one day.

Your e-mail address may no longer be free, but the small cost is well worth the investment in your long-term business.

• ▣ • ▣ • ▣ •

Kick Unprofitable Customers to the Curb

That's right, I said it, and you can quote me on it! Good customers are the lifeblood of all businesses, but bad customers can lead to a businesses' demise. Most of us—particularly those who offer services instead of products—seek loyal customers but loyalty is overpriced when it begins to consume too much time and energy—and thus destroys our profits. For example, the client that pays for one service but keeps insisting on getting another service for free. That's an expensive client. Or the client who is overly critical and impossible to satisfy. That's an annoying and stress-producing client. Or the client who acts like he's your only client—as if your entire company revolves around him. That is a business-destroying client.

To decide whether you need to sever a relationship with a client, consider how much business he actually adds to your bottom line versus how much he really costs your company—be the cost money or time spent in expensive do-overs or mediating unnecessary dramas. If you find a client is not worth the hassle, don't be afraid to let him go. Try to communicate amicably but frankly, that while you value the client, you may not be able to retain his business because of the on-going problems you have encountered.

Explain the problem succinctly and politely. If the client continues to be a headache, stop wasting your time! You can secure other less problematic clients, but only if you're willing to cut bait. Be civilized and respectful when letting a client know your services are not longer available. Don't hide behind charging inflated prices for your services in hopes of driving the client away. Rather explain respectfully that it's clear that his needs are not being met and that now would be a good time to implement a strategic change.

"Entrepreneurs have this horrifying sense of scarcity, that the customers they have are the only ones in the world," says G. Richard Shell, professor of legal studies and management at the University of Pennsylvania's Wharton School. "That is not true. But [firing clients] takes courage."

Yes, even in a bad economy, giving up an unprofitable client can be a money making idea.

• ▣ • ▣ • ▣ •

GIVE SOMETHING AWAY FOR FREE

As an entrepreneur, you must learn the power of the word *free*. Whether you use it directly or indirectly, *free* should be a regular part of your promotional efforts. Here are some ways to do so:

- *Free Promos*—When you're doing a booth at a conference or expo, don't just give away free literature about your company. It's imperative to also give away free promos, such as bags, pens, key chains, etc. The more creative your free promo is, the better. Make it memorable, and try to target the giveaway to match your audience.

- *Free Shipping*—If you sell products through your website or over the phone, the best free giveaway is the shipping cost. Free shipping is a very powerful incentive. If this poses a threat to your profitability, then consider incorporating the shipping cost into the actual price of the product. So, shipping isn't really free but you're marketing as if it is.

  Or consider offering free shipping only if the customer opts for the cheapest shipping option—usually media mail or parcel post. Studies show that offering a free shipping option can increase your sales by as much as 75 percent.

- *Free Content*—A great way to gain credibility and publicity that leads to more revenue is to give away free content. This can be done by writing a resourceful e-book and giving it away for free. This will cost you the writing time only.

You can also distribute informational columns to newspapers, magazines, and blogs, allowing them to publish them for nothing. Sites like ArticleCity.com and ArticlesBase.com are looking for free content to syndicate to thousands of publications. This, in turn, will give readers access to your insight and expertise, making them more likely to become your client.

Giving things away for free is definitely an investment. However, this investment will prove to be worthwhile in the long run. You'll find that you will generate more sales and better satisfy your customers. Even more, you'll find that in these difficult economic times you'll be able to recruit new customers who otherwise would have turned you down. Never underestimate the power of *free*.

• ▣ • ▣ • ▣ •

YOU CANNOT BUILD A BUSINESS RELATIONSHIP OVER THE PHONE

This is a very costly mistake made by entrepreneurs looking to secure long-term clients. You can *initiate* a business relationship over the phone, but you cannot effectively build one.

After you establish a potential client over the phone or through e-mail, it would be very wise to arrange to meet this person face-to-face. This can be done by connecting at an upcoming conference or networking event, or just arranging to take the client to lunch the next time you're in their city.

Keep in mind that your potential client is likely getting tons of phone calls and few actual visitors. Who do you think will stand out? The hundreds of faceless calls, or the few people who actually show up?

If you realistically expect someone to spend money with you for months or years, you must invest in the relationship. This may require you to pay for airfare, a hotel, a cab, and lunch or dinner. Some may fret over this, but if you really believe you have the products or services that the client needs, you should understand that these types of small investments will indeed pay off. Even more, if you're seeking a huge account, surely you can see that taking a $500 trip can easily be justified by the potential $100,000+ contract that you might get.

• ▣ • ▣ • ▣ •

How Entrepreneurs Can Beat the Recession

While some pundits initially called it an economic slowdown, those affected call it a full-blown recession—and rightfully so. Major airlines have folded, hundreds of thousands have lost their jobs, gas prices are through the roof, and the national foreclosure rate is at its highest ever.

In addition, small businesses across the country are drastically losing customers who no longer have money to spend with them. Black-owned companies, in particular, are affected the most. They have access to the least amount of resources to help in a situation like this, and they are often not priority enough for any federal aid.

So, what can you do to beat the recession?

- *Increase your marketing.* Buy in to low-cost solutions that are effective and will drive customers your way. Consider classified advertising, press release distribution, search-engine marketing, and directory advertising (Yellow Pages, Superpages.com, etc).

- *Consolidate your staff.* No one likes having to let people go, but sometimes you have no choice. Keep your most productive employees and have them take on more responsibility.

- *Break out the coupons and buy in bulk.* Subscribe online to receive coupons and discount offers from Office Depot, Office Max, and/or Staples to help you save money on office supplies. Also, consider buying bulk from Sam's Club, which has a special membership for small business owners.

- *Cut costs when traveling.* Instead of staying at luxurious five-star hotels like Marriott or Hyatt, consider staying at a three-star hotel like Hampton Inn, La Quinta Inn, or Comfort Inn. In addition, buy airline tickets months in advance for conferences you plan to attend.

- *Bringing staff can be very expensive.* Consider hiring someone locally where your event will be held. You can pay them for the day, and can train them on-site to work your booth.

- *Be creative.* Now is the time to really start thinking outside the box. Be unconventional. Remember that the solution to staying afloat during difficult financial times is there—you just have to find it. Meditate on new concepts and reinvent old concepts.

• ▣ • ▣ • ▣ •

IS YOUR COMPANY GREEN?

No, I'm not asking if your company is environmentally safe or if your company uses organic products. Nor am I asking if your company recycles plastic and cardboard. Those are important to do, but I'm asking whether or not your company is *money* green. Do you actually make money? Is your cash flow *flowing*?

Believe it or not, I meet minority business owners all the time who have lost sight of this very goal. They start off with the idea of generating revenue, and then they end up just casually floating around. I see them at conferences and other business gatherings. They attend just for the association. Others believe they're making money but they really aren't.

Does this describe you? If so, you need to find a way to get back on board the train of success and profitability. Thousands of African American entrepreneurs are collectively generating billions of dollars in business revenue every single year. Unless you're running a nonprofit organization, you should be generating a steady cash flow.

Here are some tips on how to keep your company green:

- *Stay focused.* If something doesn't make money for your company, minimize your time with it. Too often, entrepreneurs waste time doing things that contribute nothing to their bottom lines.

- *Stop making excuses.* Some businesses can rightfully blame the economy as to why they're not making money. More likely, the reason you're not making money now is the same reason you weren't making money when the economy was booming. Whatever the reason is, that's what you need to address.

- *Learn to adapt.* If it *is* so that your business has been highly affected by the current status of the economy, find out how people have shifted their spending habits. You may be selling something people *want*, and you may need to shift to selling something people *need*.

- *Stay in contact.* If you stay in contact with your industry leaders, you'll make more money. It happens all the time: People are handed contracts just for being at the right place at the right time, or for knowing the right person.

• ▣ • ▣ • ▣ •

FOUR MISTAKES TO AVOID WHEN RAISING START-UP MONEY

Unless you have a substantial amount of money saved to start your business, it's likely that you will need a business loan or the assistance of individual investors. Raising start-up capital is not easy; people won't simply open up their wallets for you because you say you have a terrific idea. When and if they do give you their hard-earned cash, it will be with the expectation that they will be paid back—soon. Given this reality, be strategic when raising money to launch your business. Calculate the challenges that can throw your new business into a financial tail-spin—potential pitfalls like:

1. *Showing off a weak business plan.* It won't matter if your pitch to investors sounds great when you look horrible on paper. When you meet with potential investors, i.e., people who are going to gamble on your vision (family, friends, or investment firms), make sure you're prepared. Be able to give them a carefully crafted, well-designed and thorough business plan that lays out your road map for success. If you don't invest the time and energy necessary to demonstrate how your business will succeed on paper, why should people place their bet on you? There are many resources available to assist in the creation of a bulletproof business plan. Research, write, and re-write your business plan after serious critiques by professionals. Your business is worth your very best.

2. *Not raising enough start-up money.* If you know you need $50,000 to start your business then it doesn't make sense to ask for $40,000. In fact, you should try to get $75,000 because starting a business almost always requires more money than a business owner calculates. A 2004 study published by Jessie Hagen of U.S. Bank found that 79% of businesses that failed did so as a result of starting out with insufficient capital.

3. *Having too many lenders or investors in the kitchen.* Your aim should be to target investors who can provide you with a substantial investment so you don't end up owing dozens of people. Multiple sources of money can lead to multiple headaches. Not every entrepreneur is prepared to manage competing relationships and expectations. Playing cheerleader or therapist to your investors while trying to run your business is a recipe for disaster. This is particularly true when you raise business capital from friends and family.

4. *Failing to create proper and binding legal agreements.*
   Every lender or investor wants to stake their claim on
   your goldmine when they provide you with "start-up"
   money. Make sure that all investors—including family
   members— understand the terms of your agreement,
   including how and when the money lent will be paid
   back. And don't draft the contract yourself or allow
   an investor to create one. Always seek the counsel of a
   reputable and experienced business lawyer to prepare
   a binding and fair legal agreement.

• ▣ • ▣ • ▣ •

WHAT ABOUT YOUR BUSINESS PLAN?

Often in the beginning, you don't really need a business plan
according to many self-made business successes. However, once
your business starts heading to profitability, I believe that you
can't afford not to have one. You need a viable business plan to:

- *Test the feasibility of your business idea.*
  A business plan allows you to do an initial test to
  see if your business is feasible and market ready.
  A business plan gives a detailed outline of what's
  expected. It especially shows if there's any potential
  profit to be made over the long term. There are
  numerous websites that can help you put together
  an effective business plan, as well as companies
  that assist with a plan's nuts and bolts. Having a
  professional assist you with putting a plan together
  can clarify whether or not your business has
  potential.

- *Give your new business the best possible chance of success.*
  It is integral to a business plan that financial
  objectives are clarified. A business is only as

successful as its customer service and its profit. Focus on budgeting and the market plan. These details will allow for a smoother start-up and ultimately help the business sustain itself over time. By forecasting most eventualities in your plan, you can avoid surprises and be prepared for whatever might come.

- *Secure funding, such as bank loans.*
  Most banks want to have a sense that you know exactly what you're getting into and how you're going to pay for it, before you go to them for a loan. A business plan will help them see that you have thoroughly thought through your financial needs, personal investment, and pay-back methods. Banks want to know that you're not in the dark about the financial responsibilities of running a business. A well-developed plan will show it that you're not a risk, but an asset.

- *Make your business manageable and effective.*
  A clear plan helps to ensure your business is organized, efficient, and effective. It's important to know in advance what's necessary to keep the business running smoothly. Having a plan also allows you to compare your initial vision to reality. This comparison will provide you with the data needed to not only adjust your business plan, but also to adjust your business to work better for you and your customers.

- *Attract investors.*
  Investors are always looking for new ventures to maximize their money or to help build a worthy cause. Having a stable and productive business could make you very attractive to potential investors who want to help you expand.

Investors want to see that your business is not just running well in the present, but can run well in the future. It's the future that will give them a return on their investment. A solid business plan and determined execution of it is something that will pique the interest of potential investors.

Writing a business plan takes time and effort. But in the end, it can actually ensure the success of your business.

● ▣ ● ▣ ● ▣ ●

THE LAW OF PRODUCTIVITY

The law of productivity is simple. Get things done. If you've been working all day (or all week), and you have nothing to show for it, then you lack productivity. You are not a productive worker.

Every single day, you should have something tangible to prove to yourself (and to others) that you are productive. Being productive doesn't mean that you have to have the most pivotal role in the company; it simply means you need to be contributing to the company's advancement to the next level.

Many black-owned businesses lack productivity. People show up for work, and they're doing something from 9 to 5. They're just not "producing." If what you're doing at work is not "producing" for the company, then you're wasting time and company money. Everything you do should be producing more revenue for the company—whether it's directly or indirectly.

Black CEOs must learn to keep their teams focused on this. Do not allow employees to work on meaningless tasks that aren't productive. Find something for them to do that will contribute to the company's bottom line.

For instance, I noticed that many restaurants make waiters and hostesses wrap silverware in napkins in between dealing with customers. For what? This is a meaningless task. Do the people who eat at restaurants care whether or not their silverware was wrapped up? I'm willing to bet they don't. A wait staffer can waste up to two hours a day doing this. These restaurants need to find something more meaningful and valuable for their employees to do.

I think you get my drift: Get stuff done, but get it done with a clear purpose.

• ▣ • ▣ • ▣ •

TURN YOUR CONTACTS INTO CONTRACTS

As the great power networker George Fraser says, "Turn your contacts into contracts." It's very likely that you have tons of business cards that you have collected from the last 5 (maybe 10) conferences you went to. It's also very likely that you never gave those cards a second look. Now is the time to dig up those contacts and start following up with people.

However, don't just call people randomly saying, "Remember me?" Instead, have an agenda. Be proactive, but also be productive. Ask yourself, "What are my immediate and long-term goals?" and "Who among these contacts can help me meet those goals?"

You may narrow it down to just two to three business cards, but don't be discouraged. These are the few contacts that you're going to focus on. These are the contacts that you will convert into contracts. The money is on the table—whether it's long-term money or short-term money. All you have to do is take your seat at the table and represent.

• ▣ • ▣ • ▣ •

MAKE SURE YOU'RE GETTING THE BEST PRICE

When searching to buy a new computer or office furniture, make sure that you're getting the best price. You can check your local Office Depot and Best Buy, but also check popular online retailers, such as www.Overstock.com, www.DealCatcher.com, and www.PriceGrabber.com.

Overstock.com is a very popular online destination that sells overstocked brand name items at clearance prices. They can literally save you 40 percent to 80 percent.

DealCatcher.com is basically a blog of the latest deals that various retailers are offering. For instance, they'll give you all the weekly sales and specials running at stores like Office Depot, Wal-Mart, and more. Another great site is www.Liquidation.com, an online marketplace of items that have been recently liquidated. This site is for bulk buyers only.

It's definitely worth your while to explore the possibilities at these sites before you make a small or large purchase of office furniture or the latest electronics. You could easily save yourself a bundle.

• ▣ • ▣ • ▣ •

KNOW YOUR ACRONYMS—IRA, ROI, AND RFP

You must learn usual business acronyms if you plan to be successful. The last thing you want is for someone to use a common business acronym and you have no idea what it means.

IRA — *Individual Retirement Account.* If you're an entrepreneur, you'll need to plan your own retirement.

ROI — *Return On Investment.* Whenever you invest money or services in your company, you want to have a clear understanding of what your success rate will be.

ROS — *Return On Sales* (ratio of money earned relative to total sales)

RFP   *Request For Proposal.* If someone gives you an RFP, it means that they're requesting a proposal from you. They're interested in doing business with you but want you to propose some ideas and a budget.

Other common acronyms:

B2B   Business to Business (companies that sell to other companies, like Oracle)

B2C   Business to Consumer (companies that sell to individuals, like GAP)

CAD   Computer Aided Design (design tools and software used by engineers and architects)

CAGR   Compound Annual Growth Rate (a cumulative interest rate used by investment projects or banks)

CEO   Chief Executive Officer (the big boss)

CFO   Chief Financial Officer (head of finance)

CMO   Chief Marketing Officer (head of marketing)

COO   Chief Operating Officer (head of operations)

CTO   Chief Technology Officer (responsible for the tech side)

CRM   Customer Relationship Management (a system to capture, analyze, and store customer information to manage clients efficiently)

EBITDA   Earnings Before Interests, Taxes, Depreciation and Amortization (an indicator of a company's financial performance)

EDI   Electronic Data Interchange (a set of standards used to exchange data between different companies and organizations)

EPS   Earnings Per Share (the ratio between company profits and its common shares)

ERP   Enterprise Resource Planning (a system that integrates all the data from an organization into a single location)

FIFO   First In, First Out (used both in computer programs and accounting; it determines that what comes first is handled first)

GAAP   Generally Accepted Accounting Principles (a framework used to carry out financial accounting within companies)

ICT   Information and Communication Technology (encompasses the fields related to IT and electronic communication)

ISV   Independent Software Vendor (a company or group of developers specializing in the production of software for a particular niche)

IPO   Initial Public Offering (a company's first introduction of its shares on the stock market)

LIFO   Last In, First Out (used both in computer programs and accounting; it determines that what comes last is handled first)

LLC   Limited Liability Company (a legal entity in which the owners are not personally liable)

MSRP   Manufacturer's Suggested Retail Price (a recommendation made by a company to standardize the price of its products across different markets)

NDA   Non-Disclosure Agreement (a contract between two parties to secure confidentiality)

NPV   Net Present Value (a method to evaluate long-term investments or projects)

OEM   Original Equipment Manufacturer (a company that manufacturers equipment that will be rebranded and sold by other companies; sometimes it refers to the reseller as well)

OTC   Over The Counter (trading of stocks or other derivatives directly between two persons)

P&L   Profit and Loss; also called Income Statement (an accounting report used to outline how revenues are transformed into profits)

POS	Point Of Sale (a checkout point in retail stores, or the hardware behind it)
SAAS	Software As A Service (software that is available on the web; users access it on the internet)
SOHO	Small Office/Home Office (small or home office environments)
TCO	Total Cost of Ownership (a method to estimate all the costs—direct and indirect—related to a project or purchase)
TQM	Total Quality Management (a management strategy to raise the awareness of a whole organization to quality)
TSR	Total Shareholder Return (a method of valuation that takes into consideration both dividends and share price gains)
VC	Venture Capital (capital invested in a new, usually risky enterprise; the original owners give up part of their ownership to the venture capitalist)

• ▣ • ▣ • ▣ •

FLEX YOUR BRAIN MUSCLES FOR BETTER BUSINESS RESULTS

Research shows that flexing your brain muscles can help you think faster and smarter, and can even delay the loss of memory as you get older. These are things that can benefit you as an entrepreneur in more ways than one.

You'll be able to out-think your competition, come up with more creative ideas, increase the speed of your reaction time, defuse stress, and better recall tips and strategies that you read or heard about.

Here are just a few ways to flex your brain muscles:

- *Learn how to say your ABCs backwards.* This will not only help you with your memory but will train your brain to be more flexible. It can even raise your self-esteem.

- *Start using your other hand.* If you're right-handed, learn to write and eat with your left hand and vice versa. This will help you keep both sides of your brain active, which can lead to more creative and innovative thought.

- *Learn to skate backwards.* If you like to skate, why not learn how to skate backwards? When doing so, you'll be using parts of your brain that usually never get used.

- *Exercise three to five times a week.* Regular exercise will increase blood flow throughout your body and to your brain. Running, jogging, brisk walking, lifting weights, and playing sports can all be helpful.

- *Eat brain food.* Everyone knows that fish is good brain food. Of course, the current condition of our global water and farm raised fish products supply does require that you do your homework. However, if you can locate a reliable source your brain will love you for it. Organic eggs, fruits and vegetables, seeds and nuts, and other foods with fatty acids can also improve concentration and sensory motor skills. And for a healthy dessert, try organic dark chocolate.

- *Take herbal supplements.* Fish oil, Vitamin B-6, Vitamin B-12, lithium, and Vitamin E are natural supplements that can keep your brain strong and possibly prevent your brain from aging.

- *Download some brain challenge mobile apps.* The iPhone has several applications that can help keep your brain active. My favorites are Brain Challenge, Brain Toot, and The Moron Test.

- *Use Braingle.com and BrainMetrix.com.* These are two websites that give you access to free brain teasers, riddles, trivia, exercises, games, and more.

Remember that the key to running a successful business is thinking smarter and harder. Make sure your brain is in shape to keep up.

• ▣ • ▣ • ▣ •

FROM OFFICE SPACE TO P.O. BOX

Are you one of the many entrepreneurs being forced to move out of their office spaces and back into their homes? Or have you always worked from home? Doing so almost always requires you to have a post office box as your mailing address.

Believe it or not, most entrepreneurs run their companies from home. Even before the recession, it was estimated that more than 50 percent of all small businesses did not occupy commercial office or retail space.

Despite this, small businesses collectively generate billions of dollars in annual revenue and are one of the main forces driving the U.S. economy.

So, don't be discouraged if the current economy requires you to run your business from home and list your company address as a P.O. Box. It's not unusual, or a sign of failure, and you'll be saving tons of money.

The only complication is when you have a staff. But this too can be addressed by either downsizing into a smaller, cheaper office space, or allowing your employees to work at home.

Whatever happens, know that you can run a profitable business from home. It's not something that you want to broadcast to your clients, however. Keep it to yourself. When they ask for your mailing address to mail a check, just tell them that you accept all mail through your P.O. Box. You don't have to mention that you don't have office space. You could even invest in a service that allows you to accept credit cards and checks over the phone.

Either way, you'll be fine. I've found that most clients could care less about whether or not you have office space. They're much more interested in whether or not you're providing good quality service.

● ▣ ● ▣ ● ▣ ●

WHEN TO SAY WHEN

How do you know when to give up in business? That answer is easy—never. Never, ever give up in business. But it may sometimes be reasonable to give up on a certain business idea. How do you know when it's wise to do this?

When things are consistently moving backward, not forward—this is a strong indicator that it may be time to pull the plug. Remember, it's normal to lose money in the beginning and perhaps feel like you're wasting time. But with a successful business, you should eventually start to lose less and less as time goes on.

The key is to be honest with yourself, and honest with the situation. For instance, let's say you invest $1,000 in a business idea. As time goes on, you find you have to invest $1,000 every month to keep things afloat. Over a 12-month period, not only have you not made any profit—you feel that you need to start investing $1,500 a month. This, obviously, is a business idea that needs to get axed.

On the other hand, let's use the same scenario and say that you're seeing an increasing return on your investment each month. January – $100, February – $200, March – $300, etc. This may be an idea to hold on to because by October you're going to break even and by November you'll be profitable. Even if your expenses go up, the pattern shows that you're closing the gap—and that's exactly what you want.

Never give up on an idea that shows all the signs of eventually becoming profitable. Always remember that it's common for it to take months or years to reach profitability.

There are no hard rules. However, use your judgment and learn to develop reliable entrepreneurial instincts. A true entrepreneur, although patient, is not stubborn, but instead knows when to say when. If you find that you did make a stubborn mistake, don't become a repeat offender.

● ▣ ● ▣ ● ▣ ●

NEVER CHECK E-MAIL IN THE MORNING

I was recently in a bookstore and saw a business book by Julie Morgenstern titled *Never Check E-Mail in the Morning*. I didn't even need to pick the book up because it instantly dawned on me why that's a very good idea.

Checking e-mail in the morning can wear you down before your day has even started. If you're like me, you get more than 100 e-mails every single day. The problem is that reading and scanning e-mails not only can wear on your mind but also on your eyes. Doing this in the beginning of the day only inhibits any activities that you planned for the afternoon and evening. By then, you've already sucked up your brain's juice, so to speak.

Even more, reading and replying to e-mail these days can take an hour or two or more. Before you know it you've wasted the whole morning. For most of us, the whole morning can be half our day.

The better idea is to check e-mail in the late afternoon. This way you can use your morning energy on more productive activities, such as sales calls, brainstorming, enhancing your company's services or products, strengthening your relationships with existing clients, and more.

• ▣ • ▣ • ▣ •

SHOULD YOU MIX BUSINESS WITH POLITICS?

It is typically recognized that business and politics don't mix. But it's almost unreasonable to hold that as an unequivocal truth, given that politics can have everything to do with the life of your business.

Personally, I'm neutral when it comes to politics. I'm a skeptic yet I still try to pay close attention to what's going on in the political realm so that I can be prepared for whatever changes may influence my company.

The current economy in the United States is proof positive that politics can affect the way people spend or don't spend money. Even the simplest social issue can have far-reaching effects on small and large businesses, including Fortune 500 companies.

For example, the decision to change the type of medical care in our nation inevitably trickles down to the small private practice doctor. It equally affects pharmaceutical companies, companies that provide equipment for the medical industry, those who provide paper goods for the medical industry, and businesses we may not imagine can be affected by decisions that, on the surface, seem to have nothing to do with a small business owner.

Tax decisions, cuts, increases, etc., have a direct impact on businesses across the board. How the education system is handled is yet another of dozens of political discussions that equally affect businesses.

Likewise, political decisions and legislation can affect those employees that depend on businesses large and small for their livelihood. Without workers, most companies cannot function. So business owners must pay attention to the world of politics so they can plan accordingly.

The point is this: Whether you're a political person or not, you must pay attention to what's going on in the political landscape because it can have an adverse effect on your business. Being aware and knowledgeable of potential political changes *before* they occur can keep you ahead of the competition.

• ▣ • ▣ • ▣ •

DON'T BELIEVE THE HYPE

More and more people these days are using hype to sell their products and services. I've seen this particularly with network marketing companies, who want you to join their sales team. However, I've seen it with other companies too (for example, time-share resorts, etc).

There's nothing wrong with adding a little "spice of joy" to your sales presentation. But some abuse this approach to coerce people to buy into their business concepts. My advice is to be extremely cautious of this sales tactic. For example, if a network marketer is "too happy" about you joining their sales team, something may be wrong—especially if they keep exaggerating about how much this can help your financial well-being.

Think about it. Since when are other people that concerned about your well-being? The world is much too cold to be gullible. Anyone that happy about you joining them as an associate, is often really only concerned about his/her own pockets.

What I'm saying is this: There's nothing wrong with network marketing companies and other aggressive sellers. However, if you buy into it, do so because *you* want to and because *you* believe in the products, not because you were manipulated into doing so. Also, never buy into something because you didn't want to hurt the other person's feelings. This is exactly how an aggressive seller wants you to feel.

Remember this too: A room full of people excited about a particular product or service is not necessarily a validation. This is often a sales tactic used to make you feel left out if you don't get involved.

Don't believe the hype!

Best Practices—Business Secrets

1. Remember that business is business. Never take a business deal personally—even if it goes well.

2. Don't become obsessed over one business issue; there's no need to beat a problem or challenge to death. If you can't come to terms or reach a decision on something, move on and come back to it later.

3. Don't say things that you can't prove. Be able to back up everything you say. Remember just because you saw it on the internet doesn't guarantee that the information is accurate or factual. Always double-check your sources.

4. Be honest with yourself, and your other party. Don't pretend to be something that you are not.

5. If you win a previous point, never feel like you have to give in on the next one.

6. Once you come to an agreement on one point, don't bring that point up again. Move on to the next topic of discussion.

7. Avoid getting into the habit of fighting over every little point.

8. Pay attention to what is being said. Don't have everything memorized in your head. Your responses should be related to what is actually being said.

9. Be patient and let the other parties talk. Never interrupt the person you're negotiating with.

10. Don't quit. Even if the negotiation seems to be going sour, keep negotiating.

11. Don't argue, and don't lose your cool. It will only make you look inexperienced and unprofessional.

12. Avoid arguing over small petty stuff. Stay focused on the big things.

13. Never threaten to walk away from the deal, unless you mean it. If you're not fully prepared to leave, don't even think it.

14. Under any circumstances don't ever settle for something you don't really want.

15. Don't ever let their lawyers intimidate you. You're just as smart as they are.

CHAPTER 11

FINANCE

IS YOUR FINANCIAL SITUATION SITUATED?

Starting a business is hard enough. Having credit and banking issues before you get started can make it even more difficult. Thus, the question: Is your financial situation situated?

For instance, many decide to start a business but may have bad personal credit. It would be wise and extremely helpful to clean this up beforehand. Having bad personal credit makes it nearly impossible to establish business credit, and this can be a downfall for your company.

Study your credit report, and come up with a plan to repair all your financial woes. If you owe money to a creditor who's pursuing you via a collection agency, pay it off—even if you have to do so at a rate of just $50 a month. Never give up on improving your credit score. It's well worth it, even if it takes 10 years.

Also, if you have banking history issues with agencies such as Chex Systems—you'll want to clear that up as well. Establishing a business bank account will be troublesome if you're identified as a person who has previously written bad checks or has abandoned bank accounts with negative balances.

Whatever has happened in your financial lifetime, you'll want to repair all of the squeaks. The financial world can be very forgiving if you take consistent action to fix your errors.

You don't have to be wealthy to start and build a business, but you do need a reputation that says you're responsible and trustworthy.

• ▣ • ▣ • ▣ •

FIVE STEPS FOR BLACK ENTREPRENEURS TO GET BUSINESS CREDIT

It's been estimated that fewer than 10 percent of all entrepreneurs know about or truly understand how business credit works. So, let's first define exactly what business credit is.

Having business credit means that you have a line of credit (credit cards, loans, etc.) separate from your personal credit. This essentially means that if you take out a business loan, it will only show up on your business credit report—not your personal report. In fact, anything you do regarding business credit will only affect your business.

The question is—how do you qualify for and secure business credit?

1. *Repair your personal credit.* Although they're separate, you'll probably not be able to get a line of business credit if your personal credit is bad because, initially, this is all a banker has to go on.

2. *Open a business checking account.* Be sure to do this at the same bank where your personal bank account is. This will allow the banker to see that you're a good customer. Make sure to open the account in the name of your company with a business tax ID, and try to keep at least $1,500 in the account.

3. *Approach your banker about business credit.* After months have gone by with a business account at the bank, now you can ask your banker about giving you a line of business credit. You may qualify for only $300 or even less, but take it.

4. *Utilize your credit line.* If you were approved for only $300, that's okay. Use it every month, and pay it back

every month. Within six to eight months they will likely increase it to $600 or more. Repeat the process, and one day you'll have access to thousands of dollars.

5. *Pay your bills on time.* Don't mess up your business credit. You need to pay your bills when they're due. This means keeping track of all due dates and triggering payments in advance if necessary. You can lose this line of credit just as fast as you got it. Be fiscally responsible, and you'll gain tangible business credit dividends in the long run.

● ▣ ● ▣ ● ▣ ●

SAM'S CLUB NOW OFFERING SMALL BUSINESS LOANS

There are more than 600 Sam's Club locations in the United States, and all of them are now lending centers for small business owners. The chain, owned by Wal-Mart, has teamed up with Superior Financial Group to offer loans of up to $25,000 to its small business members. And guess what? The program will focus entirely on businesses owned by minorities, women, and veterans—traditionally underserved borrowers.

This effort is one of several moves the retail giant has made to offer bank-like financial services to its extensive customer base. It also comes as the retailer tries to improve profitability at its warehouse-club chain.

If approved, applicants do not have to spend the money at Sam's Club. They can use the money as they would any other business loan. Sam's Club members who apply for a small business loan during the introductory period will receive $100 off the application fee, a 20 percent discount and a 7.5% APR, which is the term the loans will remain at for 10 years, which is common to help keep monthly payments low. There is no penalty for early repayment. For more information, call 877-675-0500 or visit www. samsclub.com.

• ▣ • ▣ • ▣ •

NEW PROGRAM OFFERS MICRO-LOANS
TO MINORITY AND WOMEN BUSINESS OWNERS

An organization called the Minority Business Loan Project is helping minority and women entrepreneurs (African Americans, Hispanics, Asian Americans, Native Americans, and women of all ethnicities) get access to micro-loans to help fund their existing or newly started businesses.

Essentially, the organization is a network of responsible lenders that specialize in helping entrepreneurs get short-term loans and cash advances up to $1,000 to sustain their cash flow.

To apply, you must be over the age of 18, have an income of at least $1,200 a month for the past 6 months or more, and must provide valid banking information to verify that you have a checking account. Those who qualify include aspiring and existing entrepreneurs, home business owners, network marketers, etc.

According to the U.S. Commerce Department's Minority Business Development Agency (MBDA) and the U.S. Census Bureau's July 2010 update, the number of minority-owned firms increased by 46 percent to 5.8 million between 2002 and 2007.

The good news from the Census? "Black, or African-American-owned businesses grew to 1.9 million firms in 2007, up 61 percent from 2002—the largest increase among all minority-owned companies; and generated $135.6 billion in gross receipts, up 53 percent from 2002."

Despite these figures, it's been reported that minority firms generate a lot a less in annual revenue and are more likely to go out of business in their first five years of existence than their white counterparts. As David A. Hinson, MBDA's National Director, said. "While the number of minority-owned businesses continues to grow, they are still smaller in size and scale compared to non-minority-owned firms." Minority firms are still less likely to be approved for business loans, business credit cards, and business lines of credit.

The Minority Business Loan Project aims to offset these disadvantages. The micro-loans are made to those who qualify, and can typically be approved within 24 hours. For more details, visit www.MinorityBizLoans.com.

• ▣ • ▣ • ▣ •

TURNED DOWN FOR A BUSINESS LOAN? CONSIDER A BUSINESS GRANT

If you've applied for a business loan in the current economy, there's a strong possibility that you were denied—even if you have good credit. This is because the current economic contraction has forced banks to be super-cautious toward all loan applicants, even if you appear to be credit worthy and responsible.

This is even worse news for minorities, who have always found it difficult to obtain business and personal loans from financial institutions. In this regard, many have turned to business grants as a solution. In 2008 alone, $360 billion dollars in grant money was awarded and more than 25% of that was given to business entrepreneurs who wanted to start or expand a business.

Though many grant programs have been reduced or eliminated by corporations and government agencies, there are still plenty of opportunities available. For instance, business grants continue to be awarded from the Small Business Administration, the Department of Commerce, the U.S. Agency for International Development, and various federal business and cooperative programs (www.federalgrants.com/Agency/Business-and-Cooperative-Programs.html), among many more. Even companies such as Miller Brewing Company, Ford Motors, and others are offering business grants through various competitions and contests.

The National Institute of Business Grants (www.BusinessGrants.com) is encouraging entrepreneurs and small business owners to persist in their efforts to seek financial support by redirecting their search toward business grants.

Helpful resources include:

- *www.Grants.gov*—a central storehouse for information on more than 1,000 grant programs that provides access to billions in annual awards

- *www.BusinessGrants.com*—a useful reference to learn about frequently asked questions pertaining to business grants

- *www.Business.gov/guides/finance/financing*—a directory of local and national business financing programs

• ▣ • ▣ • ▣ •

WHY BUSINESS GRANTS WILL NEVER GO OUT OF STYLE

Business grants were originally created by federal and local governments to provide financial assistance to entrepreneurs and business owners. The goal was and still is to help stimulate the national and local economy, and to help fund research that will help a certain industry. In more recent years, non-profit organizations and major corporations began to give out business grants. They had similar goals, but also found that giving away grant money is good for public relations and is a handy tax write-off.

For nearly 100 years now, business grants have helped thousands of individuals across the country either start or expand a business. Some business grants have even provided free tools and services (software, hardware, consulting, coaching, etc.) to underrepresented minorities and disadvantaged women who want to start businesses.

Many are now concerned that a bad economy might lead to the end of business grants. They reason that companies will no longer be able to afford to give money away, and that government agencies will reallocate funds to more pressing priorities. That reasoning is mostly false.

The good thing about business grants is that, unlike business loans, they'll never go out of style. Remember that business loans are given by companies eager to tap into the research and development energies of entrepreneurs and small businesses to make a profit. Business grants, on the other hand, are given as deductible charitable gifts. Their availability is not as dependent on the economy, and because they were never designed to be re-paid—they don't and never did pose any risk to the grantor. Even further, business grants are great tax write-offs for major corpo-rations—especially if they're in financial trouble. Granted, some companies will reduce the amount of grants they give out—but they generally won't terminate the program completely.

Government agencies may also reallocate some of the funds that normally go for business grants, but their business grant pro-grams will always exist. This is because local and federal govern-ment officials realize that small businesses drive the economy and create jobs. They can't afford to destroy programs that can help small businesses thrive—especially as they frequently face re-elec-tion during a recession.

Here are the top five misconceptions and why you should completely ignore them:

- *Business grants aren't real,* Of course, they're real. This can easily be verified by going to www.Grants.gov— a government-sponsored website that reveals all the federally funded grant opportunities available. Even more, you can check with your local (city, county, and state) officials to find out about their grant opportunities.

- *Business grants are given only to people with business degrees.* This couldn't be further from the truth. Very few grant opportunities require that you have a business degree. In fact, many of them don't even require that you have business experience.

- *Business grants aren't given to minorities.* Wrong again. There are tons of grants that are designed for minority-owned businesses. Even more, women are considered a minority too—and there are plenty of grants for women.

- *Business grants are too hard to get.* Obtaining a business grant does require some work, and definitely some patience. It can involve a lengthy application, some tedious modifications to your business plan, and even some face-to-face meetings. However, the potential payoff for your labor is well worth the effort.

- *Funding for business grants has been drastically reduced.* Reduced, yes. Drastically, no. What funding doesn't get reduced in a bad economy? Despite this, there are still tons of opportunities available. So stop making excuses, and go get them.

Don't give up your search for the business grant that's right for you. They're still out there, and many entrepreneurs are receiving such assistance every single year. To find relevant opportunities, remember to check the websites of relevant major companies and smaller companies. You also want to check with your local city, county, and state government offices.

The National Institute of Business Grants provides free tips and information not widely known on how to obtain business grants. For more details, visit www.BusinessGrants.org.

• ▣ • ▣ • ▣ •

HOW TO GET MINORITY BUSINESS GRANTS

Winning a minority business grant isn't an effortless enterprise. But with a little determination, finding the grant you need for your business can be easier than you think. There are numerous places to search, including the Internet and your local library.

Organizations that specialize in helping businesses, such as the Small Business Administration (SBA), have a wealth of information to assist small business owners with everything from business registration to grants. The SBA will guide business owners through the sea of information, taking the time to ensure the road to a productive business doesn't turn into a nightmare.

The government also specializes in grants and loans to assist every aspect of a business. www.Grants.gov is one of many resources that provides grants for various organizations, including small businesses. Another, www.USA.gov, also gives small business financial assistance to businesses that qualify.

There are numerous local government organizations that provide grants and loans to businesses within a particular field. For example, the U.S. Fish and Wildlife Service provides grants for related businesses. Its objective is to help build a particular business in an effort to build or revitalize a dwindling or threatened resource.

Each state has valuable resources for minority business owners. Local governments typically set aside a portion of their funds for grants to help build a city or state. These funds are a huge part of building economic viability in a particular area, ensuring there are enough jobs and resources for the people. Most major corporations in these areas also have a foundation that specifically provides funds for various outside projects related to its social or political values. Research Fortune 500 companies and you might be surprised to discover that most of them provide funding for a host of initiatives.

Don't forget to visit your local library. There are dozens of books that give detailed listings of every foundation in existence, as well as grant opportunities nationally. There ARE grants out there for minority businesses. You just need to commit to doing the research required to find them.

Here are some additional resources:

- Minority Business Development Agency— www.mbda.gov

- National Minority Business Council—www.nmbc.org

- Minority Business Entrepreneur Magazine— www.mbemag.com

- Grants For Women—www.GrantsForWomen.org

• ▣ • ▣ • ▣ •

Annual Listing of Business Grant Opportunities

The National Institute of Small Business Grants, a leading global resource for business funding, publishes an annual listing of business grant opportunities. This extensive compendium is available online at www.BusinessGrants.org, and is free to the public.

Nike, Microsoft, Intuit, Pepsi, MillerCoors, and IBM are just a few of the companies listed that have programs designed to give business grants away this year. Organizations include the Bill and Melinda Gates Foundation, Dayton Foundation, IFA Educational Foundation and the PepsiCo Foundation. Government agencies include the Federal Aviation Administration (FAA), the Federal Transit Administration (FTA), the United States Department of Agriculture (USDA), and more.

Because the Internet is saturated with so much fraudulent information pertaining to business grants, BusinessGrants.org was launched in 2008 as the official online resource for legitimate funding opportunities. The site reports on all avenues of business funding, and features exclusive and original news, tips, videos, and a daily blog.

The National Institute of Small Business Grants (NISBG) has recently expanded its efforts to educate entrepreneurs and is now taking advantage of social media to reach more people. In addition to its resourceful website, it has launched a daily blog, a YouTube channel, and a Twitter account.

The blog (blog.businessgrants.org) publishes daily news, commentary, and tips pertaining to business grants. Readers can subscribe free via e-mail and RSS to receive daily content that will help them better understand the grant-making process. Users can leave comments, questions, etc.

YouTube (www.youtube.com/businessgrants) features the latest online videos on how to obtain business funding. This unique collection offers hands-on training on how to obtain business grants, loans, and venture capital. There are also interviews with various finance experts, and news coverage of relevant happenings in Washington.

The Twitter account, @BizGrants features daily tweets and retweets of recent articles and press releases related to business finance and funding. Users can also use this to be updated about upcoming events, and to ask questions or leave comments.

For more details, visit www.BusinessGrants.org

• ▣ • ▣ • ▣ •

WHEN BUSINESS GRANTS ATTACK: HOW TO AVOID THE SCAMS

In a time when banks and credit unions are denying loan applications like never before, many entrepreneurs and business owners are turning to business grants as a dependable source of financial help. However, just like scholarships and other financial aid opportunities—be aware of the sounds-too-good-to-be-true scams.

Here are the top five signs of a business grant scam:

1. *No phone number listed.* If you're on the website of an organization or government agency that's offering a business grant opportunity, make sure that there's a working phone number listed. If not, it's probably not a legit outfit. There should also be a working e-mail address listed.

2. *P.O. box address.* A P.O. box address associated with a business grant indicates it may be a scam. But don't assume—be sure to investigate because some organizations have physical addresses but want all correspondence to go to a mail box.

3. *Fee required.* If a company or organization asks for your credit card number or requires you to send a money

order with your application, this will almost always indicate a scam.

But remember that it's very normal for some companies to charge a fee for you to access their grant database. Others will charge a fee to send you a CD-Rom or e-book. This is okay. What's not okay is you having to pay to *apply* for an individual business grant opportunity.

4. *Poor website design.* If you visit a website promoting a grant opportunity, and the design looks poor and elementary—it's likely a scam. Organizations and government agencies that give grants away have professional-looking and well-developed websites.

5. *Sounds too good to be true.* If an organization is making far-fetched statements about a grant opportunity, it's more than likely not legit. For instance, some grant opportunities may say "We can give you $1 million dollars for your business," or "No application is ever denied." These are claims that indicate a bogus operation.

● ▣ ● ▣ ● ▣ ●

HOW TO GET GOVERNMENT CONTRACTS

Federal contracts are the Holy Grail to those awarded them and the American Idol dream of those who compete for them. In order to win the federal contracting game you have to know the rules and the regulations. Opportunities for small businesses in the government sector are real if you have enough motivation and discipline to learn to play the game with skill. That will take time and energy. Sharon McLoone's informative *New York Times* article on exactly how to get a government contract is a great place to begin your research. Here are a few of my favorite McLoone highlights:

- Of the more than 20 million small businesses in the United States, only about 500,000 are currently in a position to do business with the federal government. That's not because they are the only ones capable of doing the work; it's because they know how to get the work.

- Here's how big the opportunity is: small companies are eligible to bid on any size contract, but the government is required to reserve all federal purchases between $3,000 and $100,000 for small businesses—unless the contracting officer can't get offers from two or more small businesses that are competitive on price, quality and delivery.

- Think micro. Almost 300,000 government employees are authorized to make purchases that total as much as $3,000 through the SmartPay program. No contracts required.

So are you ready to play the game to win? If the answer is yes, consider finding a SCORE mentor with government contract experience and develop contract winning skills.

• ▣ • ▣ • ▣ •

Brass Tacks

WERE YOU BROKE WHEN THE ECONOMY WAS GOOD?

Many people were struggling financially when the economy was booming and are still struggling now. Suddenly, though, they feel very comfortable blaming their situation on the bad economy.

Conduct an honest self-evaluation. Are you broke because of the bad economy or because of the following other reasons?

1. Mismanaging money

   Problem: Some people are very guilty of overspending on unnecessary items. Others have no idea what a budget is.

   Solution: Write down all your transactions, and total them up at the end of the month. It sounds tedious, but in two months you'll realize how much money you waste. $300 on fast food, $250 on video games, $500 on clothes. You'll be a changed person forever.

2. Mismanaging your personal credit

   Problem: Many have ruined their credit with unpaid bills and loans, late payments, bankruptcies, and more. Now they can't even buy a car (let alone a house) without paying a 20% interest rate.

   Solution: Get a copy of your credit report and a calendar, and come up with a three- to five-year plan to fix your credit. Call your lenders and tell them you're serious about paying them back, and ask them to reduce what you owe. Many times, they'll comply. Remember that just $50 a month for four years can pay off $2,400 worth of debt.

3. Not learning a trade or skill

   Problem: Many never took advantage of the opportunity to attend college or learn a trade. Now they're stuck with minimum wage jobs and no expertise to start a company of their own.

Solution: Discover what skills you are naturally good at, and teach yourself more. Find the right books, take an online class, earn a certification if possible, and get rolling. It's never too late to start.

4. Not saving money

Problem: Too often, people don't put money away. Many don't even have savings accounts, let alone a retirement plan.

Solution: It may be sunny for a while, but one day it will rain. Hard times are inevitable. Put as much money as possible away, so that when you need it—it will be there. Think about it: Had you done this five years ago, you'd probably have a little bit of money to get you through this bad economy. Open up a savings account today, and use it.

● ▣ ● ▣ ● ▣ ●

RECESSION-PROOF YOUR BUSINESS

The recession has negatively impacted businesses both small and large. Many have been forced to close their doors and others that haven't are struggling to stay open. However, despite the down economy, many are actually thriving. It's interesting to note that while Washington Mutual was going through bank failure, JP Morgan Chase was able to expand and acquire them. Likewise, Wells Fargo and Citibank had enough money in their reserves to bid on Wachovia Bank when it was going under. In a failing economy, how is it that some banks were going out of business, while others were doing so well that they could make billion dollar acquisitions? The answer is simple. The ones going out of business were not prepared for the economic crisis.

What about you? Is your company—or one you plan to start—prepared for a down economy? If not, you need to recession-proof your business. To accomplish this goal consider offering products needed during both good and bad times. For example, people will still pay to have their cars and computers fixed even when things are tight, but they probably won't buy a car or computer unless they have to. Just as important, make sure your services or products are affordable. Consider the good business of lowering your prices to bring in more customers and offering them discounts to make sure they return.

Another key to remaining recession proof is to watch your spending. Many new business owners make the mistake of spending their profits on unnecessary personal items instead of saving funds or re-investing in their businesses. Wait until you have surplus money in the bank and your loans are paid off or down before you spend your extra cash reserves.

Finally, don't expand until you are absolutely ready. If you need one room for your store, don't rent two rooms just to make your business look larger—one day you might not be able to afford it. Or if you plan to start selling cell phones then stick with that effort until it's successful before branching out into other merchandise. Forcing your business to grow prematurely and spending extra money to expand can backfire in a poor economy. They key is to allow your business to grow naturally.

• ▣ • ▣ • ▣ •

ARE YOUR BOOK, DVD, OR CD PRICES TOO HIGH?

I consult and coach a lot of aspiring authors, and it always surprises me when first-time authors or musical artists sell their books for $25. This is very expensive pricing for a hardcover book—especially when it's written by unknown authors or experts. Even a $20 price tag can be just too much.

Consider the recent wake-up call that the book publishing industry received from Amazon.com, the world's biggest bookseller.

In July 2010, Amazon announced that it is now selling more digital hardcover books on Kindle than traditional hardcovers. From March to May 2010, Amazon sold 143 Kindle books for every 100 hardcover books. However, in June 2010, Amazon sold 180 Kindle books for every 100 hardcover books. The digital revolution is just beginning. So it's time for all savvy self-published authors to reconsider the marketplace that once supported $20 trade paperback originals when Kindle can distribute digital products instantly at $9.99.

I've also witnessed entrepreneurs selling their independent DVDs, CDs, etc., for way too much money. Sadly, these business owners lose countless sales because in the current economy potential customers have to think twice and ask themselves if the entertainment item is worth the price.

Consider the prices for your services and products? Are they too high? Are you losing customers because they feel you're too expensive? The best way to price whatever it is you're selling is to look at your competition, and go lower. If your competition is digital, you have to consider what value-add a traditional hardcover or DVD or an enhanced digital edition can add to your customer's experience. Don't get hung up on the idea of making a fixed percentage profit per sale. Which would you prefer—to make a $1 profit on thousands of individual sales, or to make a $5 profit on eight sales? Meditate on the Wal-Mart model. If you under price your item to a competitive level and take a lower profit margin—you'll make up for it in volume.

Make sure to experiment with pricing the first time around—before you launch your promotional campaign. If people visit your website and feel your prices are too high, they won't come back after you realize your mistake and decide to lower the price. You have to close the sale on their initial inquiry.

• ▣ • ▣ • ▣ •

A Small Profit Margin Can Be Huge

Many entrepreneurs will turn down a business opportunity because the profit margin seems too small. Sometimes this is a good reason to walk away. But sometimes it may be a reason to jump on board. In many scenarios, a small profit margin can mean huge returns because of volume.

Believe it or not, many Fortune 500 companies have very small profit margins. It's quite common for a major corporation to generate a billion dollars in revenue and net only 20% or 200 million.

Many would say that 20% is too low, but they're focusing on the fact that 80% of the revenue is lost. First off, the 80% is not lost. It takes money to make money, and the 20% left over is still substantial.

Even if a company operates with a 10% profit margin, this can be a lot. For instance, if your company generates $1 million in revenue at a 10% margin—you still walk away with $100,000 in profit. That may sound like it's significantly less, but it's a whole lot more profit than most companies ever see.

Remember, too, that what you pay yourself on payroll can be included among your expenses. So your personal income is not part of what the company nets, which in a sense raises a 10% profit margin to 15% or 20%—depending on your personal salary.

• ▣ • ▣ • ▣ •

The Down Side of Not Upselling

Upselling is simple. If someone comes in your restaurant to buy a hamburger, you encourage them to also buy some fries. If someone comes to your barbershop to get a haircut, you encourage them to also get a facial shave. If someone comes to your website to buy a new desk, you encourage them to also buy a new chair.

Like I said, upselling is simple. So simple, that it is responsible for billions of dollars in extra revenue for business owners. If you're not upselling, you're losing big because many times customers will impulsively accept your offer. The key is to make the offer sound irrefutable.

For instance, if you're selling a product for $100, feature a $25 upsell. $125 vs. $100 for the total order doesn't sound like much of a difference to the customer. But for you, it can create an extra hundred or thousand dollars in monthly revenue.

If your prices are smaller, you can still use this concept. For instance, if you're selling a product for $20, you can feature a $5 upsell. Again, $25 vs. $20 for the total order won't seem like much of an increase to the customer. But for you, it can be mean a significant increase in revenue.

If your business is strictly online, it's very effective to feature the upsell options on the checkout page. For example, "Would you like to add the following product to your order for just $5 more?"

Experiment with upselling and see what happens. It'll be well worth your time to at least attempt to make this work—whether you're selling products or services.

• ▣ • ▣ • ▣ •

THE "HOOK-UP" HURTS BLACK ENTREPRENEURS GROWTH AND PROFITABILITY

Long ago, it was discovered that African Americans often don't support black-owned businesses. Sadly, one major reason is because too many people want the "hook-up." Instead of paying for products and services, they want them free or for a drastically reduced price, whether it be family, friends, or sometimes even colleagues.

Alfred Edmond, Jr., editor-in-chief of BlackEnterprise.com, wrote a memorable column about this phenomenon:

> One of the biggest drags on black entrepreneurial growth and profitability is the "hook-up": black people expecting other black people to provide them with free goods and services just because they're black. We need to stop it. Today.

I completely agree. I've observed this business liability in action more times than I care to count. From free food to free tickets to free books and every other form of the proverbial "free ride." Too often friends, family, and acquaintances forget that the whole point of being in business is to make money. Instead of supporting black-owned business enterprises, they want us to start living large before we've even hit lift-off by soliciting the freebie. Not only does this hinder a black-owned business from growing, but it can also make them go out of business fast.

Consider this alternative to the hook-up. Create special VIP discount coupons or passes for friends and family. Explain that they are truly VIPs because they are committed to helping you create a strong foundation for your business or professional services. Take the time to educate your VIP customers to understand that you're in business and that you appreciate their support. When friends and family members understand the inestimable value of "hooking you up" through their word-of-mouth support for your business—everybody wins.

Finance—Business Secrets

1. Learn about business grants at www.BusinessGrants. org or www.business.gov/finance/financing/grants

2. Learn about President Obama's ARC loan program for small businesses at www.ARC-Loans.com or www.sba. gov/recovery/arcloanprogram/index.html

3. To get a business credit card, business loan, or business line of credit—you have to fix up your personal credit. No bank will give you business credit if your personal credit is jacked up!

4. Consider going to a community bank when applying for a business loan. Every year, nearly 100 new community banks open their doors—and many of these are very business friendly.

5. Whenever you apply for a business loan, ask your bank about SBA loans. They usually charge less in interest, and can be approved faster. If your bank is not an SBA lender, find one that is.

6. CreditCards.com is an online marketplace that helps you find, compare, and apply for business credit cards.

7. Save money when leasing a car for your company by going to SwapALease.com. This website allows you to take over other people's vehicle leases. The cars are always new, in great shape, and you don't need to make a down payment.

8. MillerCoors hosts an annual business grant competition called the Urban Entrepreneur Series for minority-owned companies. Every year, they give away four grants for $25,000 and one for $50,000. For more details, visit www.MillerUrbanEntrepreneurs. com

9. Visit the Minority Business Development's Agency website at www.MBDA.gov for a listing of state resources and financial assistance available to small and minority businesses.

10. Be careful about finance companies that target minority business owners and charge high interest rates. This is a form of predatory lending that unfortunately is not illegal. Always be 100% clear about the terms of any loan.

11. Many believe that business grants are given away by the federal government. This is false. It's actually the city, county, and state governments or private companies that give away business grants. Check with your local officials. Also, check with major companies and non-profits that are headquartered near you.

12. You can't claim your whole house as a tax-deductible business expense, unless you use your whole house for business. Otherwise, you can only claim a percentage of the home. For example, 1/4th or 1/3rd. If you claim the whole house, it will likely cause problems on your business taxes.

CHAPTER 12

MARKETING AND ADVERTISING

EVERY COMPANY IS A MARKETING COMPANY

To succeed in business, entrepreneurs must attract and retain a growing base of satisfied customers. This means that business owners must come up with a way to convince people to try out or keep using their particular products or services. This is where marketing comes in.

Marketing is based on the importance of customers to a business. Every company, regardless of its product, is a marketing company. I don't care if you own a flower shop or an investment firm, or what your company sells or produces—at the end of the day, you're a marketing company. All company policies and activities should be directed toward satisfying customer needs, and you won't sell anything if you have no way to let potential customers know you exist.

This means that you need to spend at least 50 percent of your time and money on marketing—promoting whatever it is that you do. Too often, black entrepreneurs get into the habit of *not* self-promoting. This is the worst mistake to make in business.

In addition, remember that you want to market to *new customers*. There's nothing wrong with revisiting past clients to stimulate continuous business activity. However, new customers should constantly be flowing to your company.

Marketing is more than just passing out flyers and business cards, or putting an ad in local newspapers. Marketing is about realistically assessing how you're going to get a constant flow of potential customers. You need to brainstorm and come up with clever and impressive ideas. Do something that no one else is doing. Reinvent the wheel. Be spontaneous and innovative. Make it your goal to recruit at least one new customer each week. As time goes on, you can up the ante to one new customer every day.

To give you the right perspective, think about this: companies like Allstate and Verizon never stop running commercials on TV. In fact, on any given day, you'll see their advertisements on TV, in magazines, on billboards, and more. By doing this, they sign up thousands of new PAYING customers every single day of the year (including Sundays).

The conclusion is straightforward: If you want to generate more revenue, you have to invest constantly in your marketing initiatives. That's the secret!

• ▣ • ▣ • ▣ •

MARKETING IS A SCIENCE

Marketing is indeed a science. It's all about conducting experiments based on educated guesses. This involves market research, assessment, and experiments. Some say that marketing is an art because it's all about selling. But it's not all about selling. Marketing is mostly about research, thus the term "market research." When the proper research has been done, the product will sell itself.

One marketing professional once commented, "When you begin to formulate the type of marketing you will do, it involves the gathering of massive statistics. These stats, from validating a media buy to formulating the right message, sending graphics to the right audiences, are science at its best."

So what does this mean for entrepreneurs? Well, it means you should do two things when launching a marketing campaign:

- *Study or research your potential customers before you market to them.* Do focus groups and conduct surveys to identify what customers think about products and services. Don't make any assumptions. For instance, don't conclude that just because there are a lot of kids in your neighborhood that starting an ice cream store is ideal.

- *Experiment with different methods of marketing to consumers.* Passing out flyers and business cards may or may not work for what you're promoting. However, you won't know if other avenues (newspaper ads, event sponsorship, postcard marketing, etc.) work until you try.

Just like any other science, marketing has no rigid rules. There is plenty to be discovered. Push the boundaries, open new doors, and find what works for you! Think outside the box. Create another box if you have to.

• ▣ • ▣ • ▣ •

WHY 90 PERCENT OF THE PEOPLE I MARKET TO BUY WHAT I'M SELLING

Over the past 10 years, I've been able to figure out how to get 90 percent of the people whom I target to buy into my BlackPR. com service. That's right, my conversions are 90%—and I'm not exaggerating. It did require some trial and error, but it's not that difficult to do.

Here's how you can do it too:

- *Make your product a necessity.* Create a product or service that people need. They'll want it if they need it. Remember that everybody needs something, including non-profit organizations, government agencies, and other businesses. There are always voids that need to be filled—even in a bad economy.

Second, *make sure that you mark*et only to the people who need your products or services. This can be very challenging, but work hard to find a way to specifically and exclusively reach your intended audience.

- *Keep it simple.* Your website, your promotional material, your approach, and your service/product should all be simple. Complicate these things, and your results will also be complicated.

  The fewer pages on your website, the better! My site, BlackPR.com, is a one-page website that has generated more than $1 million in revenue over the past four years.

  Minimize the amount of text you use to describe your products or services because a picture *is* worth a thousand words, and remember testimonials speak volumes.

- *Be persistent.* This is the most important step. Being persistent in your marketing efforts separates you from the people who fail in business. Once you find the people who need your product or service, you should literally market to them nonstop until their lawyer sends you a cease-and-desist letter.

  Don't annoy them every day or every week with spam and junk mail. Instead, create a noninvasive, no-pressure, balanced marketing campaign that combines e-mail, social media, postcard marketing, event marketing, and offline networking. In your persistence, your aim should be to become a resource to them—someone who is knowledgeable and respectable in the industry.

If you apply these three suggestions in the right way, I guarantee that 90 percent of the people you market to will buy what you're selling.

• ▣ • ▣ • ▣ •

Put Some "Stimulus" in Your Marketing Plan

It's no question that we live in difficult economic times. People are losing jobs every day, and more and more companies are going out of business. Among all this chaos, it's very common to hear certain words and phrases, such as "recession," "economic stimulus," "bailout," and even "recovery."

Why not implement these words in your marketing plan? If they're designed to make the American people feel hopeful about the U.S. economy, imagine how it could make your customers feel about doing business with you.

For instance, I launched a "PR Stimulus Package" theme to help market my BlackPR.com service in the midst of the economic downturn. The theme was displayed on the website, included in an e-mail blast to our clients, and was the tag line on the 5,000 postcards that we mailed out. The concept was to encourage people to "stimulate" their PR efforts by using our service to distribute a press release to the black media.

I experimented with other phrases, such as "PR Bailout" or even "PR Recovery," but decided that "PR Stimulus" had the widest appeal.

Other companies from different industries can utilize comparable themes in a similar way. For example, if your company offers a credit repair service—you can launch a "Credit Bailout" or a "Credit Stimulus" campaign. Or if you own a restaurant, you can launch a "Taste Bud Stimulus" campaign.

Obviously, such themes won't work for every company. The point is to be creative, and try to be innovative with your marketing efforts. Consumers love to be marketed to in a fun but relevant way.

• ▣ • ▣ • ▣ •

"IF YOU BUILD IT, THEY WILL COME"—IS THIS TRUE?

Most of us are familiar with the popular movie *Field of Dreams* starring Kevin Costner. The 1989 film is best known for the voices that whispered, "If you build it, they will come." The statement was made to Costner's character, encouraging him to build a baseball field in his backyard to get dead baseball legends to come and play.

Those words were so popular that, 20 years later, many still use the phrase to emphasize to others that you have to build on what you believe in. They tell aspiring entrepreneurs that "If you build it [your company]...they [the customers] will come."

Is this true? Can you simply build a company and expect customers to show up? Absolutely not. You have to do much more than just build a company. To get those customers, you have to actually brand and market your company.

Think of it this way: How did you find out about the products you currently buy? Nine times out of ten you either saw a commercial on TV, heard it on the radio, saw it in a magazine, clipped a coupon from a newspaper, saw a banner ad, or got an e-mail promo. You also may have heard about it via word-of-mouth from someone else who learned about it through those outlets.

The point is that you did not telepathically come to know that a certain product existed, and that you could buy it. You were marketed to, and this is exactly what you must do to promote your own services and products.

Whether you're selling a book, opening a coffee shop, or starting a lawn care business—you must understand that customers will not just automatically show up at your door. They don't know you exist until you market to them. You can spend $1,000 on your website, $200 on business cards, and $500 on equipment—and still end up with no customers.

Early on, you must factor in what your marketing strategy will be and create a budget for it. If your marketing initiatives are not realistic or just plain non-existent, I promise you—you'll fail. If you believe (as so many do) that you'll automatically get customers when you start your company, the only thing you will get is automatic failure.

I'm changing the aphorism, right here and right now. My updated version of the classic is: "If you build it and market it, they will come."

• ▣ • ▣ • ▣ •

DON'T WAIT FOR THE PHONE TO RING

As an entrepreneur, you cannot sit around waiting for people to discover you. You have to be proactive and go get your clients. If you don't, someone else will.

Utilize services such as Jigsaw.com, SalesGenie.com, or even YellowPages.com to find your prospects.

Once you've identified one, cold call them or send them promotional material through the mail. Remember that people generally don't mind a sales pitch, as long as its relevant to what they do.

Don't be intimidated by size, either. Big Fortune 500 companies like Coca-Cola, Verizon, and Marriott do business with smaller companies all the time. Most of them even have supplier diversity programs and they allocate a certain percentage of contracts to minority companies. This is where you fit in, so don't hesitate to reach out to them.

Stop making excuses. The opportunities are out there. You just have to go after them—relentlessly. Get on the phone and start making contacts. In the words of Tommy Lasorda, "The difference between the impossible and the possible lies in a man's determination." You have two options in business: you can either win or lose. So, play to win!

• ▣ • ▣ • ▣ •

Is Your Business in High DEF?

I'm not talking about visual effects, pixels, or resolution. I'm not talking about Blu-Ray, VGA, DVI, HDMI, plasma or LCD TVs at all.

I'm talking about DEF (Demand, Efficiency, and Frequency). Your business should always be in high demand, operating with high efficiency, and involved in a high-frequency marketing program.

Here are some tips:

D *Demand*: To increase the demand for your company, your services and products should be designed to solve people's problems. Come up with ways to make people feel they need you and cannot operate without you. Create a buzz and learn how to keep people talking. Remember that up to 80% of your business can come from word-of-mouth referrals.

E *Efficiency:* To increase the effectiveness of your company, you must learn to be efficient—no wasted time, effort, or money. Especially during a recession, you want to make sure that all of your company's energy is spent profitably. Find out what works and step it up. Find out what doesn't work and stop doing it.

F *Frequency:* To increase the frequency of your company's brand recognition, you must launch a regular and consistent marketing program. I strongly recommend that you engage in some type of marketing every single day. The more frequently people see your company, the more likely they are to buy your product or service.

• ▣ • ▣ • ▣ •

LACK OF DIVERSITY—A CLASSIC MISTAKE

It still shocks me that many companies don't embrace diversity of any sort in their marketing and advertising campaigns. In fact, it baffles me.

The total U.S. population reported by the U. S. Census in 2008 was 304.1 million, that total includes millions who are members of a minority group. Today's America is populated by 46.9 million Hispanics, 37.6 million African Americans, about 13.4 million Asian Americans, and another 2.4 million American Indians or Alaskan Natives.

Recently, I was watching late night TV and noticed two companies that seemed to be out of step with America's growing diversity. One was Hydroxycut and the other was GetARoom.com—both of who have several commercials that feature only white actors and models. Don't get me wrong, I'm not trying to single out these two companies. There are plenty of others that do the exact same thing.

I'm just perplexed as to why they wouldn't recognize that including minorities in their ads is good business. Research shows that minorities respond favorably to advertising that features people that look like them. Since more than 35 percent of the country is made up of minority citizens, it's puzzling why any company would not want to tap in to this market share.

Do the folks at Hydroxycut think that minority people don't want to lose weight? Do the folks at GetARoom.com think that minority people don't stay in hotels? Or are they both too underexposed to understand that the world is changing and still incorrectly think that they can capture all audiences without taking a more diverse approach?

Seriously, this is basic stuff—Diversity Marketing 101.

• ▣ • ▣ • ▣ •

THE POWER OF VIRAL MARKETING

Viral marketing is a phenomenon that facilitates and encourages people to pass along a marketing message. This type of promotion, also known as word-of-mouth advertising, has been deemed the most effective marketing method.

According to Blake Rohrbacher, a writer for The ClickZ Network, a client will eventually tell at least 12 other people about their good or bad experience with your company.

This translates into two things for you:

1. *Take care of your customers:* The last thing you need is for one of your customers to be bad-mouthing your company to others. Twelve people is quite a bit, so be sure to keep your clientele satisfied. Happy customers will say good things about you and encourage others to utilize your services.

2. *Invest in viral marketing:* Now that you know the power of viral marketing, perhaps you can invest some time and money into it. Give your customers something to talk about, and encourage them to share their experience with friends and family.

If you have a local business, get it listed on Yelp.com and encourage your customers to submit online reviews for others to see. Local businesses with storefronts should give customers coupons and/or referral materials to pass along.

Above all, understand the power of viral marketing on the Internet. Take advantage of social networks like YouTube.com, MySpace.com, Linkedin.com, BlackPlanet.com, and HBCUConnect.com. These sites are extremely "viral." If you're part of them—your brand will be heavily exposed.

If possible, reward your customers for sending you new clients. This can easily turn the typical 12 referrals into 30 or 40.

• ▣ • ▣ • ▣ •

NINETY PERCENT OF YOUR POTENTIAL CUSTOMERS SHOULD RESPOND TO YOUR ADVERTISING

Many would disagree, but I believe that 90 percent of your potential customers should respond to your advertising. They may not necessarily buy from you, but they should respond by either visiting your website or contacting you for more details.

If this cannot be said of your marketing campaign, it could be for one of these reasons:

- *You're targeting the wrong audience.* Marketing to a broad, general audience is a classic mistake that many companies make. Every product and service appeals most to a specific group. Find out who they are, and find a creative way to target them in your marketing. Remember that not everyone is a potential customer—just the people within this group.

- *You're selling the wrong product.* If you're marketing unsuccessfully to a very targeted audience that should have an interest in your product or service, it could be that your product or service doesn't cut it. No one ever wants to believe this, but it's true in many cases. Conduct some market research, and ask your potential buyers for honest opinions. Even the most unique products and services can be neither wanted nor needed by potential customers.

- *Your pricing is off.* If your price is too high, people will feel they can't afford it—even if they can. If your prices are too low, people will feel that your products or services might not be of good quality. Experiment and find the price that people are comfortable with.

- *Your presentation is weak.* If your presentation is unprofessional or amateur-looking, it doesn't matter what you're selling—people won't buy it. Your website, brochures and business cards absolutely must look modern and professional. Even if your actual products and services are up-to-par, consumers will penalize you greatly if your presentation looks like garbage. If you're not a professional graphic designer, don't design your own materials.

● ▣ ● ▣ ● ▣ ●

WHAT DO GLADE®, RAID®, ZIPLOC®, AND WINDEX® HAVE IN COMMON?

The answer is simple. Not only are they all very big brands worldwide, they're also all owned by the same company—S.C. Johnson & Family, which also owns and produces Oust®, Pledge®, Shout®, and many others. Notably, each of these brands individually generates hundreds of millions of dollars in annual revenue.

I've always been impressed by the way S.C. Johnson & Company was able to create a line of products that people use during their entire lives. Even more impressive is the fact that some of their brands are so big that people use them commonly enough to appear in the dictionary.

For instance, many people will refer to all glass cleaners as *Windex*. Others will refer to any bug killer as *Raid*. I find this market dominance amazing and am truly impressed when a company accomplishes this.

That, however, is the power of branding, and all businesses (big or small) should attempt to create some type of brand recognition for their products and services. Make sure that you have a professionally designed logo and a short name that's easy for people to recall and pronounce. In addition, remember to standardize the colors on all your marketing materials.

True, S.C. Johnson spends hundreds of millions of dollars each year in television and print advertising, but this is not the only way to succeed. The key is to constantly promote your brand with the resources you have. Every month, you should have some type of active marketing program in place. Press releases, classified ads, web banner ads, conference booths/exhibits and postcard marketing campaigns, are great ways to inexpensively keep your brand alive.

• ▣ • ▣ • ▣ •

SEND OUT A WEEKLY OR MONTHLY NEWSLETTER TO YOUR CUSTOMERS

Stop making excuses about creating a newsletter! It's now easier than ever to create, maintain, and distribute one. And who said anything about a print newsletter?

All you have to do is create an account with ConstantContact.com or VerticalResponse.com—in seconds you can be sending e-mail newsletters. These services are very user-friendly.

My company has distributed two to three different newsletters every single week since the year 2001. I am 100 percent convinced that this is what has kept us in business.

• ▣ • ▣ • ▣ •

JUNK MAIL HAS A PURPOSE

Ever wonder why you keep getting the same old junk mail in your mailbox? It's because advertising through junk mail actually works! Think about it: Direct mail marketing to millions of people every single day or week can be very expensive. Why would companies do this if it weren't effective?

The truth is that people (at home or at work) actually look at junk mail, and will respond if they see fit. So why not launch a small postcard marketing campaign to your potential or existing customers? It only costs $.28 to mail a postcard, but through bulk rates they can be as low as $.19 each.

Why not run a small test to see what happens? That's what I did five years ago, and now I'm a postcard marketing addict. To launch your test postcard marketing campaign, I recommend using 48hourprint.com or ModernPostcard.com. Both printing services are fast and have reasonable prices.

• ▣ • ▣ • ▣ •

FIVE REASONS WHY YOUR MARKETING IDEAS DON'T WORK

1. *You don't know what marketing is.* Many people have only a general understanding of marketing. They fail to realize the differences between advertising and public relations. They don't fully understand buzz marketing, guerilla marketing, referral marketing, or even online marketing.

2. *You don't brainstorm enough about marketing.* When most people think of marketing, they think of passing out flyers and sending an e-mail to all their friends. Marketing goes far beyond this.

    It involves brainstorming and experimenting to see what works and what doesn't. Essentially, there are no rules—you just have to be creative, think of new concepts, and give them a shot. If one idea doesn't work, move onto another.

3. *Your promo materials and website are too wordy.* I've seen this a million times, and it irks me every time. Be economical with words. People don't want to read an essay when they get your brochure or visit your site.

    Keep it simple, and keep it short. Try to use an outline style of writing, and remember that people don't read—they scan.

4. *Your promo materials and website are poorly designed.* If you're not a graphic designer or website developer, it's in your best interest to hire someone. Having poorly designed brochures, flyers, postcards, business cards, etc., is a great way to turn a potential customer away. Having a bad-looking website is even worse.

Your materials and website don't have to look perfect, but they should look professional and modern.

5. *You don't spend enough on marketing.* I've found that most new entrepreneurs who complain that marketing doesn't work will only spend about $25 a month on promoting their products or services. Some spend nothing at all.

   Of all your business expenses, marketing is *the* most important. No matter how good your product is, people will never buy it if they're not aware it exists. So allocate sufficient funds in that area.

If these statements describe you, there are tons of books written on these topics. Visit your local library or bookstore and find the book that best addresses your company's goals. Again, marketing is the most important component to running a business. It is well worth the investment of time, energy, and money.

● ▣ ● ▣ ● ▣ ●

"SUPPORT ME, SUPPORT ME"

Is your idea of marketing your business to contact your friends and relatives and pressure them through guilt to support you?

Sadly, this practice is very common. Entrepreneurs and network marketers don't realize that by doing this, they end up annoying people and making it even less likely to get a favorable response.

The truth is, your products and services should sell themselves. Potential customers (including family and friends) should be naturally inclined to do business with you. If you've pressured people through guilt to buy what you're selling, you're probably in the wrong business.

Develop creative marketing and PR campaigns. Research how to make the most of a shoestring advertising budget. Roy H. Williams of *Entrepreneur* magazine says there are four things to remember when operating on a shoestring ad budget:

1. *Time and money are interchangeable. You can always save on one by spending more of the other.* I have a young mechanic friend who specializes in older model BMWs. In his glove compartment are several dozen 5-by-7 fliers that say, "I specialize in fixing BMWs just like this one. Is it running like it should?" Whenever work is slow, he drives through big parking lots with hundreds of cars and looks for older BMWs. When he finds one, he slips the flier under the windshield wiper after scribbling a personalized note to the owner, such as "Arctic blue has always been my favorite color on this model. You should be proud of it." He usually begins getting calls on his cell phone while he's still out distributing fliers.

2. *High rent accomplishes the same thing as advertising. It gives you exposure.* Is there a place you could be where people could see you at work? Imagine the volume of business a shoe repairer could do at a kiosk in the mall. After seeing him at work once or twice, hundreds of people would begin tossing their old shoes into the car whenever they were headed to the mall. Why isn't anyone doing this?

3. *The cost of giving away a sample is often less expensive than the cost of advertising.* Free samples are often cheaper than advertising. The cost of free sampling is incremental. If no one responds to your offer, it costs you nothing. If it costs you a lot, it's only because it worked well. What are you waiting for?

4. *In the end, it's what you say in your ad that matters most. So say something irresistible.* When you have a small ad budget, it's especially important that you make a compelling offer. There's no "right people to reach" when you're saying something that no one cares about. I've never seen a business fail because it was

reaching the wrong people. But I've seen hundreds fail because they were saying the wrong thing.

Learn about the wonderful benefits of grassroots marketing. According to *Inc.* magazine's website, if "you're not Procter & Gamble or Volkswagen," grassroots marketing can be an "effective way to spread the word about [your] business and retain customers without spending a fortune . . . Roxanne Quimby, the CEO of Burt's Bees, didn't fight fire with fire. Instead, she relied on good old-fashioned word-of-mouth marketing to raise the profile of her products . . . The company invests heavily in producing and distributing samples and uses its retail locations as key figures in its marketing efforts.

Low-cost or no-cost guerrilla marketing is a useful tool for small businesspeople and entrepreneurs because they must employ smarter rather than harder ways to promote and advertise. Guerrilla marketers must use all of their contacts to network, find creative publicity stories, angles, and outlets, and generate ideas that'll get noticed and talked about. Some examples of guerilla marketing are:

- A business owner associating himself as an expert on a current event so he can get quoted in the media

- An entrepreneur nominating herself for an award and promoting her nomination and receipt of the award (if she gets it)

Experiment with social media tools such as Facebook, online radio services such as BlogTalkRadio, and even video outlets such as YouTube, to help promote your business.

Find or create a business opportunity that sells something people can't resist—something they really want, really need, or both. You should only be selling products and services that people will buy without pleading and begging. Whatever you do, come up with something better than "If you care about me, you'll buy something."

• ▣ • ▣ • ▣ •

ARE $1 COUPONS ENOUGH?

I was just recently at the post office the other day and a guy's passing out $1-off coupons for a local barbershop. I think to myself, "What the heck are you doing? Why would I (or anybody else) visit your barbershop to take advantage of a measly $1 discount? Nearly everyone who gets haircuts already belongs to a barbershop of some sort. And your game plan to get them to switch to yours is to save $1?"

Don't get me wrong. A $1 coupon is worthwhile if I'm going to the grocery store to buy some $2 waffles. That's a 50 percent discount. Even if I were at the mall buying some $3 sunglasses, $1 off is a 33 percent discount. But $1 off a haircut is an insult. Haircuts these days cost at least $15, but sometimes up to $20. So handing me a $1-off coupon is only offering me a saving of about five percent or less. That's not enough to motivate anyone to take action.

If you're going to use coupons or discounts in your marketing strategy, make sure to make people feel that they're actually getting a bargain. Ideally, the saving should be at least 15 percent—but never below 10 percent. The greater the saving, the better the response you'll get. If done correctly, you'll always make up any loss through the increase in new customers.

• ▣ • ▣ • ▣ •

INCREASING YOUR ADVERTISING DURING A RECESSION REALLY WORKS

At the beginning of the economic downturn, I wrote a blog about how entrepreneurs can beat the recession. My very first point in that article was to increase your marketing effort—something that has been reiterated over and over by business experts. Well, I practiced what I preached and it worked!

I had every indication that November and December 2009 would be extremely slow months for my company. Despite this, they turned out to be extremely profitable months and December turned out to be the best December my company has had in the past eight years.

The strategy was to blitz my existing and potential customers with tons of helpful tips and advice so they'd see me as a dependable resource. This, in turn, would encourage them to buy my services, specifically, to increase transactions for my BlackPR.com, BlackExperts.com, and BlackSpeakers.com services.

Here's a list of the top ten things I did:

1. Attended, networked, and had a booth at *Black Enterprise*'s conference in Charlotte, FraserNet's conference in Atlanta, and the Diversity Business conference in Orlando.

2. Attended, networked, and spoke as a panelist at the African American Internet conference in Chicago, at the Turning Point Urban Business Summit in Los Angeles, and at the Junior Black Chamber of Commerce National Conference in Los Angeles.

3. Attended and was a keynote speaker at the Booker T. Washington Economic Development Summit in Tuskegee, Alabama.

4. Increased my budget allocated to online advertising through Google Adsense, Yahoo Marketing, and Adbrite.

5. Sent out direct marketing postcards to all 3,000 of my previous and existing clients—encouraging them to use our services again.

6. Began e-mailing all my clients to encourage them to use our services more frequently.

7. Compiled a list of influential people, and started sending them our company press releases on a biweekly basis.

8. Started reaching out to my biggest clients to create a personal relationship with them. I even met with some of them and took them to lunch.

9. Blogged more frequently on DanteLee.com.

10. Created a Twitter account (www.twitter.com/DanteLee)
    and started using it on a daily basis.

As you can probably suspect, I had to spend quite a bit of
money and time on each and every one of these areas. But it was
well worth it. Not only did I make a 400 percent return on what I
invested, but I ended up with more than 120 new clients.

All those back-to-back conferences worked extremely well—
that's where we recruited a lot of our new clients. The other strategies helped a lot with branding and turning existing followers
into paying customers. For instance, I was able to convince the
majority of the people who follow my blog to buy my services.

When the economy contracts, increase your marketing activity. It really does work!

• ▣ • ▣ • ▣ •

AFFILIATE REVENUE IS REAL

Surprisingly, most African American entrepreneurs are not involved with affiliate marketing. Many aren't even aware of what it
is. Affiliate marketing is when you promote an advertiser's services
or products on your website. In exchange, the advertiser pays you
a commission every time a lead or sale is generated from your
website. The concept is called CPA (Cost per Action) Advertising.

Sounds simple, but believe it or not: The affiliate marketing industry generates billions of dollars in annual revenue for people
(like me and you) who have websites. Because everything is on
a pay-per-performance basis, it is completely free and easy to get
started. To get involved, you can sign up at an affiliate marketplace
like Websponsors.com or Hydramedia.com (my personal favorite).
The key is to find offers that match the content of your website. For
instance, if you have a site focused on health, it would make sense
to run offers from health insurance providers who will pay you
up to $20 per quote that you generate. If your website focuses on

education, it would make sense to run offers from colleges who will pay you up to $35 every time a student requests more information.

Affiliate marketing is a great way to generate revenue from your website, especially when you're having trouble convincing advertisers to pay you up front.

Some affiliate programs, like Google Adsense, will pay you whenever someone clicks on your ad, whether they complete an action or not. This is called PPC or Pay-per-Click. The concept is huge and very real. I've been doing it for about 10 years. In 2008 I made nearly $200,000 from affiliate marketing.

Here are my stats:

Rextopia.com	$32,000
AKMG.com	$9,700
HydraNetwork.com	$89,000
Google Adsense	$52,000
CJ.com	$5,100
VCMleads.com	$10,000
Total	$197,800

This looks like a lot of money, but it is only pennies on the dollar. I know people who are doing $200,000 to $500,000 a month in affiliate revenue. The key is that your website has to get a lot of traffic, and you have to find relevant affiliate programs that cater to your audience. You also have to find ways to creatively promote the offers to your audience.

Plan to attend events that focus on affiliate marketing, such as Ad Tech (www.ad-tech.com) and Affiliate Summit (www.affiliate-summit.com). Their conferences are usually held in New York, San Francisco, Miami, Las Vegas, Boston, and Chicago. The workshops are very helpful, and they have an expo where you can meet and interact with a lot of affiliate marketing and internet technology companies.

Also, subscribe to *Revenue* magazine (www.revenuetoday. com)—a very good publication that reports on affiliate marketing trends and opportunities. My goal in 2011 is to double or triple my affiliate revenue. I plan to do more research, more networking, and get more traffic to my sites. There's too much money out there, and I want a bigger piece of the pie.

●　▣　●　▣　●　▣　●

BUT WAIT! ORDER RIGHT NOW AND WE'LL THROW IN A FREE . . .

Likely, you've heard that phrase while watching a late night commercial or infomercial. It's very commonly used, and believe it or not—it actually works. By simply giving potential customers a sense of urgency via an incentive, that technique has helped create a very lucrative $100 billion infomercial industry. The marketing companies behind these infomercials are very aware of impulse buying, and how easy it is to get consumers engaged. The funny thing is, few people would admit to being an impulse buyer—although most of us are and don't realize it.

So how can you apply this to your business? Well, don't be intimidated by the idea of paying for expensive airtime because television isn't the only place to launch such a campaign. You can do it right from your website, and even at your storefront or conference booth. I highly recommend that you read the book *But Wait...There's More! Tighten Your Abs, Make Millions, and Learn How the $100 Billion Infomercial Industry Sold Us Everything but the Kitchen Sink* by Remy Stern.

But Wait dissects the direct-response marketing business and reveals how the televisual format originally came from traditional sales pitches. That's right! The same techniques used in infomercials came from old school sales practices.

When reading the book, be sure to try and creatively come up with ways to inexpensively apply the suggestions to your business.

• ▣ • ▣ • ▣ •

MARKETERS: U.S. AFRICANS DIFFER GREATLY FROM AFRICAN AMERICANS

A study by New American Dimensions and the African Chamber of Commerce finds that many African immigrants living in the U.S. maintain their cultural traditions. Marketers beware—not all black-skinned consumers living in the U.S. fall into the demographic segment commonly referred to as African American. African immigrants are a separate and unique group that is growing in number in the U.S. These consumers maintain connections to friends and family in their home countries as well as their ties to native traditions, including food, music, and entertainment.

These insights come from an exciting new comprehensive study by Los Angeles-based multicultural research firm New American Dimensions in conjunction with The African Chamber of Commerce, Dr. Bruce Corrie and Aguilar Productions. From multiple focus groups in Los Angeles, New York City and Minneapolis to a quantitative survey of 393 African immigrant adults, this study captures unique insights into the daily lives and thoughts of this highly educated and successful group. The study is supplemented by a video snapshot of Africans to personify the findings from the research and bring them to life.

Highlights of the study, available at www.newamericandimensions.com, include:

- African immigrants are ambitious and hard working.

- Success is often described in meaningful, far-reaching terms.

- Half of the respondents say that Africans are completely different from African Americans or blacks.

- Many surround themselves with diverse and primarily international friendships.

- Respondents voiced absolute commitment to their families and children, noting that this was a top African value.

- Many respondents immigrated for education in the U.S.

- Respondents expressed disappointment with the portrayal of Africans in the media.

"There are over 1.4 million Africans living in the U.S. and these consumers possess very high educational attainment and incomes. Additionally, this is a segment with a powerful sense of identity and pride in being African," said David Morse, president and CEO of New American Dimensions, a firm that provides customized multicultural consumer research.

• ▣ • ▣ • ▣ •

WHAT IS MARKETING RESEARCH?

It's impossible to sell products or services that customers do not want. Learning what customers want and how to present it attractively is what marketing research is all about. According to the American Marketing Association, marketing research is "the systematic gathering, recording, and analyzing of data about problems relating to the marketing of goods and services." It is not a perfect science, since it deals with people and their constantly changing feelings and behaviors—which are further influenced by countless other subjective factors.

Without being aware of it, most business owners do marketing research every day: analyzing returned items, asking former customers why they've switched, looking at competitors' prices. Most small business owners have a sense of their customers' needs from years of experience, but this informal information may not be timely or relevant to the current market. In this way, a small business has an edge over a larger one because a large business must hire experts to study the mass market, while a small-scale entrepreneur is close to the customers and can learn much more quickly about their buying habits.

To conduct marketing research you must gather facts and opinions in an orderly, objective way to find out what people want to buy, not just what you want to sell them. The U.S. Small Business Administration has provided some useful marketing resources for small business owners. Here are some questions that will help you to begin effectively doing your marketing research:

- Who are my customers and potential customers?

- What kind of people are they?

- Where do they live?

- Can and will they buy?

- Am I offering the kinds of goods or services they want at the best place, at the best time, and in the right amounts?

- Are my prices consistent with what buyers view as the product's value?

- Are my promotional programs working?

- What do customers think of my business?

- How does my business compare with my competitors'?

Market research, like other components of marketing, such as advertising, can be quite simple or very complex. There are various ways to conduct simple market research, such as including a questionnaire in your customer bills or using online survey software, such as surveymonkey.com, to gather demographic information about your customers. Regardless of the simplicity or complexity of your project, you'll benefit by including market research as part of your overall marketing strategy.

Marketing and Advertising—Business Secrets

1. Submit press releases through BlackPR.com, an extensive press release distribution service to all the African American newspapers, magazines, TV, and radio stations—over 1,000 news outlets. Distribute press releases or columns at least once a month to get publicity for your company.

2. Submit press releases through PRweb.com, a press release distribution service to mainstream media via search-engine optimization. This service is a great way to get traffic to your website and publicity for your business.

3. Launch a $250–$500 scholarship contest. This is a great way to draw attention to your company and get a lot of free publicity. Scholarships are passed around quite a bit, and it's a great way to make people aware of your brand. Be sure to submit your scholarship opportunities to sites like FastWeb.com and Scholarships.com.

4. Consider advertising with AdBrite.com. It allows you to promote your website via text links, banners, and full-page ads that appear on other websites within their network.

5. List your company on SalesVantage.com, a popular online directory of vendors for advertising, marketing, sales training, telemarketing, event planning, and web services.

6. If your company sells actual products, list them for free in the Google Product Search. You'll get tons of free traffic and orders. For more info, visit www.google.com/base/help/sellongoogle.html.

7. Long form sales letters work. Have you ever gone to a website and realized that it's nothing more than a one-page sales letter? You scroll down only to see about 50 paragraphs full of rhetorical questions, descriptions, testimonials, sub-headings, and postscripts. This is known to outperform short copy, sometimes by as much as 400 percent. Experiment with this technique immediately.

8. Article marketing is a very effective way to get traffic to your website and enhance your search-engine optimization. The concept is to write relevant articles pertaining to your industry, and to mention your company and website briefly at the bottom in your tag line. ArticleMarketer.com offers a great service that distributes your articles to thousands of websites.

9. Invest in learning about marketing and research. When the proper research has been done, the product will sell itself. For a terrific list of free online marketing courses from institutions ranging from MIT's Sloan School of Management to University of California, Irvine and the SBA check out http://educationportal.com/articles/10_Places_to_Find_Free_Marketing_Courses_Online.html.

10. Research your potential customers before you market to them. Do focus groups and conduct surveys to identify what customers think about products and services. Make no assumptions. For instance, don't conclude that just because there are a lot of kids in your neighborhood that starting an ice cream store is ideal. Surveymonkey.com is useful for conducting research and focus groups. It's an online tool that enables you to conduct, manage, and analyze research as well as publish online surveys, and view results graphically and in real time.

11. A great way to put yourself in front of an audience is to volunteer to speak or give a presentation at a conference. Many conferences will be glad to have you because the success of their event depends on good speakers sharing good information.

12. Join a speaker's bureau. It will get you speaking engagements, and you can use your speaking opportunities to promote your company. You can develop your public speaking skills through organizations like Toastmasters International, an organization that teaches public speaking and leadership skills through a worldwide network or the National Speakers Association (NSA), the leading organization for professional speakers. For more information go to www.toastmasters.org or http://www.nsaspeaker.org/.

13. Use BizBrag.com to post news, send e-mails, and chat about what's going on in your business. It's a great way to publicize yourself to other entrepreneurs and business owners.

14. "Free is the new paid." This may not work for every business, but try giving your products and services away for free for just one day. If you're a restaurant, give away food. If you're a bookstore, give away 50 books. Make sure you publicize it, and it should generate a buzz.

15. Advertise on Google—the most popular search-engine in the world. You can bid on key words, and have your ad show up only when those key words are searched. For more detail, visit www.Google.com/adwords.

16. Advertise on Yahoo. Your business will show up in their search results and on other popular sites. Like Google, you can bid on key words and pay only when

someone clicks on your ad. For more detail, visit http://searchmarketing.yahoo.com.

17. Advertising on MSN and Bing.com. Similar to Google and Yahoo, your ads will show up in search results on a pay-per-click model. For more detail visit http://adcenter.microsoft.com.

18. Advertise on Facebook, the social network used by over 200 million people around the world. You can kick off an ad campaign on their site for just $50 to $100. Even better, you can target your ads to appear only to people of a certain demographic. For instance, if you want your ad to be viewed only by women age 45–65 who live in Houston, Miami, and Detroit who like to watch "Sex and the City"—you can do that. For more detail visit www.Facebook.com/ads.

19. Advertise on MySpace, a huge website that allows millions to host their own web page for free. You can kick off an ad campaign for $50 to $100 and target it to a demographic of your choosing. For more detail visit http://advertise.myspace.com.

20. Advertise on LinkedIn, the largest online community for professionals with a household income of $109,000. The site is used by millions of career-driven and business-savvy men and women. For only $50 to $100, you can start advertising to a group of people that match a description of your choice. For more detail visit www.linkedin.com/directads.

CHAPTER 13

PUBLIC RELATIONS

WHAT DOES PR MEAN TO YOU?

The most common meaning of PR is "public relations." It is defined as "the practice of managing the flow of information between an organization or individual and the public, gaining them exposure to their audiences using topics of public interest and news items that do not require direct payment for advertising."

However, PR can also mean "press release"—an official statement distributed to the media to supplement or replace an oral presentation. A series of press releases can be very helpful in managing a company's or individual's public relations campaign.

PR can even mean "people relations"—just a different way of describing public relations, with more emphasis on the fact that the public consists of actual people.

To some, PR just means "phone ringing"—by which a public relations campaign is launched to increase phone calls to a sales number where consumers can order products. Or the goal could be to get journalists to call to ask questions and schedule radio and TV interviews.

To others, PR means "plenty of requests"—when a campaign is launched to increase website traffic and have potential customers inquire via e-mail or online.

To all, however, PR really just means one thing—"profitable results." Whether your campaign consists of just press releases or a combination of media strategies—the goal is always to help your company or organization produce more revenue. When done correctly, that's exactly what PR will do.

• ▣ • ▣ • ▣ •

PROMOTE, PROMOTE, PROMOTE

At a recent diversity business conference I was chatting with a marketing director from Merrill Lynch, which had not long before lost billions as a result of the national foreclosure crisis. I asked him if this would affect the advertising budget. He told me "no" and that they were planning to increase their spending.

Research confirms that in times of an economic slowdown, many big businesses *increase* their advertising budgets. If so, how much more important is it for small businesses to increase their promotional efforts? Now is a great time to have a better presence at conferences, to launch a postcard marketing campaign, and even to solicit speaking engagements at industry events. Now is the time to give away free T-shirts and other promotional items with your logo.

Promotion is so much more than just passing out flyers and business cards. It's so much more than just running a classified ad in the local newspaper, or even sticking a magnet on your car. Effective promotion requires actual legwork. Become a make-it-happen entrepreneur, get on your feet, and get those clients. If you have a booth at an expo, don't just sit there. Engage people. Conquer the masses, and recruit them as long-term customers.

Don't use the bad economy as an excuse for your business being slow. Things can easily speed back up when you take an active hands-on role in your company's advertising methods.

• ▣ • ▣ • ▣ •

"I SEE YOUR NAME EVERYWHERE"

There's nothing more satisfying to an entrepreneur than to hear someone say those words to you. It's a dream come true. I've had this comment made to me on numerous occasions by some very notable people, and it definitely makes you feel like you're doing your job. That's when you can be certain that all those PR tactics you've been working on over the past few months or years are actually working.

If you have yet to receive this kind of positive feedback, here are some things to do:

- Recognize that public relations is central to your marketing success. Yes, people should know about your brand, but they should also know about the person behind the brand—you.

- In many cases, consumers are more apt to buy into what your company is selling if they know and respect the face of the company. This is also why celebrity endorsements work so well. People recognize a face and gain confidence in the product.

- Include your name, face and quotable information in all your marketing efforts. A professional headshot and brief profile should always be featured on the "About Us" section of your website. Make sure that you're quoted and your brand is referenced on your press releases and marketing materials (brochures, media kits, etc.)

- In self-promotion, always err on the side of taste and balance. Be mindful about oversaturating yourself. Never discredit yourself by inflated self-promotion. The key is to find a balanced way to skillfully integrate yourself into your company's image.

- *I See Your Name Everywhere* by Pam Lontos. This book has a perfect title, and was authored by the perfect writer. Lontos is an industry veteran who runs a very successful public relations firm in Orlando. Her book is filled with tons of useful PR strategies.

• ▣ • ▣ • ▣ •

RECESSION STRATEGY: SPEAK YOUR MIND

People are always hungry for valuable information from a respectable voice. This is where YOU come in. You're an expert, a guru, a genius—and people are just waiting to hear what your opinions, thoughts, and ideas are.

The best way to meet this demand is to write relevant columns and distribute them to the media. For instance, if you're a business coach, write about how the economy is affecting small businesses and what you would do about it. If you're a health practitioner, write about your solution to a current health issue, such as the spread of swine flu. If you're a technologist, write about the latest technological development in your area and why you think it's huge. If you just authored a book about love and relationships, write about love and relationships.

How does this help you? Well, many newspapers and magazines will print your columns for free, and many radio stations will want you to come on-air to further discuss the topic. This, my friend, is free advertising for you. By doing this, you draw attention to yourself and your company. But remember to avoid self-promotion within the body of the column or interview. This is seen as very unprofessional. You want to remain unbiased, and mention your company, services, and contact info briefly at the very bottom of your column in your tag line.

When you've finished writing your column, forward it to all your colleagues and ask them to forward it to all their colleagues. Depending on your budget, consider distributing your columns as actual press releases through newswire services, such as BlackPR. com and PRweb.com.

If done correctly, writing good columns regularly (weekly or monthly) will lead to more publicity for your business—and more revenue.

When you write your columns, be sure to include your tagline. A tagline is a few explanatory lines at the end of your column that includes a brief bio: who you are, what you do and, if appropriate a link to your website. When distributing your columns, be sure to fax and/or e-mail them to the correct editors at various media outlets. Be sure to specifically target publications and journalists that are related to your industry. For instance, don't send a sports-related column to a health journalist.

Always post your columns to free sites, like ArticleCity.com, Helium.com, ArticlesBases.com, and GoArticles.com. These are websites that thousands of editors and publishers go to when looking for free content. Doing any combination of these suggestions will almost guarantee you free publicity. Your phone should start ringing, and you should be able to drive more traffic to your website to sell more of your products, services, books, DVDs, etc. The key to making this a success comes down to three words: *High Quality Content*. If you take the time to invest in some meaningful, juicy content, you'll reap the benefits almost overnight.

• ▣ • ▣ • ▣ •

BE CONTROVERSIAL

One of the hardest things to do in public relations is to get people's attention. Controversy usually gets people's attention. Dare to be edgy or debatable. According to David Frey of MarketingBestPractices.com and writer of *The Power of Controversy Marketing*, "Controversy not only gets other people's attention, it also gets the media's attention. The media knows that *people love controversy* and so they jump at the chance to cover controversial topics." That's what publicity is all about.

The news industry thrives on controversy because that's what readers and viewers like. Whenever there's controversy, news ratings go sky high. So don't shy away from creating a situation where some people love you and some hate you. Come up with a way to put your company in the limelight. In his 18-page online guide, Frey offers five methods for creating "a storm of controversy":

- Go against a long-held belief.

- Disagree with a noted expert.

- Align yourself with a controversial topic or event.

- Report on a controversial topic.

- Do something controversial or very unusual.

Controversy can generate free publicity and word-of-mouth advertising, and there isn't a single business that cannot benefit from this kind of PR. It usually works best when you're selling consumer products to the general public. It may sound a bit difficult, but such publicity can translate into millions of dollars of free advertising.

· ▣ · ▣ · ▣ ·

YOU ARE YOUR OWN BEST PR

You are your own best PR, so ask yourself, "How do people see me?" People should view you as a helpful resource, not an aggressive salesman. Instead of being a walking billboard, be a walking encyclopedia. Once you figure out this concept, you'll see your sales skyrocket because consumers are motivated to buy from people who know—or appear to know—what they're talking about. For instance, if you're selling insurance, you should be writing weekly columns and blogs to educate people about financial literacy, wealth, and other related issues.

Hold regular, free seminars for people to attend, and free tele-seminars for people to call. You should be sitting on a board of advisors. If you're establishing yourself in your field, volunteer for committee roles in your professional organization. Consider producing free audio/video content on BlogTalkRadio or YouTube, and offer some type of free consultation. Most importantly, you should be the author of at least one book that's related to your expertise. Start by writing e-books and give them away for free. If people see you as an informative asset, not just a pushy salesman, they'll buy everything you're selling. Even more, they'll refer you to all their friends and family members.

● ▣ ● ▣ ● ▣ ●

ARE YOU READY TO BE "GOOGLED"?

Every single day, millions and millions of people use search-engines to find what they're looking for. It is very likely that, at some point or another, someone will be searching for information about you. Being researched, or "googled," can be very good or very bad. It all depends on what comes up when your name is typed in. Fortunately, you do have some control over the matter. Here are some things you can do:

- *Regularly send out press releases.* Search-engines love press releases and news content. Whenever you send out PR, it will usually be indexed right away from the distribution company itself and any online news outlet that publishes it. PRweb.com and BlackPR.com are great tools for this.

- *Get listed in online directories.* Search-engines will generally give content from business directories a higher ranking. This is because information from such sources is viewed as "official." Therefore, listing your bio and/or company description on these sites can help to authenticate what's "official" about you. Sites like Business.com, SalesVantage.com, and BlackExperts.com (another one of my services) are perfect examples.

- *Make sure your website is search-engine friendly.* If you "google" your company's name, your company's website should come up first. If it doesn't, you need to optimize your website so that search-engines are able to crawl through the content.

- *Be careful about MySpace/BlackPlanet blogs.* Remember, if someone "googles" you, everything will come up—everything. So, if you have a MySpace page with pictures of you acting the fool—you may want to delete it or make it a private blog. You don't want potential clients to change their minds about your company because they stumbled upon your personal MySpace revelations.

• ▣ • ▣ • ▣ •

DON'T JUST HAND OUT BUSINESS CARDS

Stop being a business card distributor. You know who you are. You go to all the networking events with a stack of cards and pass them out like flyers. Not only are you wasting your time, but you're also wasting your cards. Instead of randomly passing out business cards, talk to people and find out if they're actually interested in what you offer. In addition, focus on getting others' business cards so you can follow up with them later. Don't depend on people to follow up with you.

The average person will not keep your business card (no matter how creative the design), so it's your responsibility to keep theirs. Doing this will enable you to make contact via e-mail, phone, or direct mail marketing. I promise you that you'll close the circuit much more often if you implement this simple strategy.

• ▣ • ▣ • ▣ •

How to Get a Standing Ovation

Guy Kawasaki of *Entrepreneur* magazine recently outlined several points on delivering a successful speech and getting a standing ovation. Here are just a few:

- *Have something interesting to say.* This is 80 percent of the effort. If you have nothing to say, don't speak—end of discussion. It's better to decline the opportunity so no one knows you don't have anything to say than it is to make the speech and prove it.

- *Cut the sales pitch.* The purpose of most keynote speeches is to entertain and inform and seldom to provide you with an opportunity to pitch. For example, if you're invited to speak about the future of digital music, don't talk about the latest MP3 player your company is selling.

- *Focus on entertaining.* Many speech coaches will disagree, but the goal of a speech is to entertain the audience. If you do, you can slip in a few nuggets of information. But if your speech is dull, no amount of information will compensate. If I had to pick between entertaining and informing an audience, I'd pick entertaining, knowing that informing will probably happen too.

- *Understand the audience.* If you can prove to your audience in the first five minutes that you understand who they are, you've got them for the rest of the speech. All you need to understand are the trends, competition and key issues facing your listeners. This simply requires consultation with the host organization and a willingness to customize your introductory remarks.

- *Tell stories.* The best way to relax when giving a speech is to tell stories—any stories: about your youth, your customers, etc. When you tell a story, you lose yourself in the storytelling. You're not "making a speech" anymore. You're simply having a conversation. Good speakers are good storytellers; great speakers tell stories that support their message.

- *Circulate with the audience before the speech.* Heighten the audience's connection with you by talking with them before you go to the microphone— especially the ones in the first rows. When you get to the podium, you'll see these friendly faces. Your confidence will soar, you'll relax, and you'll be great.

- *Practice often and speak all the time.* This is a "duh-ism" but nonetheless relevant. My theory is that you have to give a speech at least 20 times to get decent at it. You can give it 19 times to your dog if you like, but it takes practice and repetition. There's no shortcut to Carnegie Hall. As renowned violinist Jascha Heifetz once said, "If I don't practice for one day, I know it. If I don't practice for two days, the critics know it. If I don't practice for three days, the audience knows it."

• ▣ • ▣ • ▣ •

"BE THE MEDIA"

Be The Media by David Mathison is a great book that helps in-dependent bloggers, authors, and entrepreneurs create and distrib-ute content without giving away their royalties, rights, or souls in the process. It's deemed the "ultimate independent media hand-book."

Filled with 536 well-written pages of research, guidelines, and critical suggestions on how to maximize media exposure and rev-enue while minimizing your budget, this title is a must-have for every 21st century entrepreneur. Interestingly enough, the book is NOT available at Amazon.com or other online retailers because that would defeat the message of selling independently and keeping more of the profit.

This is easily the best book I've seen on this topic. The text presents invaluable research, and it offers relevant and up-to-date reference material on best technology and media practices.

Mathison, a well-respected and internationally recognized media expert with more than 20 years' experience, was recently featured at the 2010 National Speakers Association (NSA) convention, where he discussed "how to leverage social media to move fans from conversation to engagement—to help you sell more products, earn more revenue and get more gigs—without professional PR." This media entrepreneur engaged his audiences so brilliantly that he sold 5,000 copies of his book in 11 days, an accomplishment that got him featured in *The New York Times* and helped him leverage countless speaking engagements.

I highly recommend this book. Its research is invaluable and it offers relevant and up-to-date reference material. To purchase, visit www.BeTheMedia.com and check out Mathison's proposed affiliate program to see if it holds any product synergy for your website.

• ▣ • ▣ • ▣ •

WHY YOUR PRESS RELEASE DIDN'T WORK

First, you can't assume that your press release didn't work because you didn't hear from anybody. Many newspapers and magazines will publish your press release without telling you. Second, many radio stations will briefly mention the content of your press release on the air without telling you. Generally, you're contacted only if there's a problem with your press release, if you're needed for an interview, or if there are some unanswered questions.

With all that said, it's still possible for a press release to simply not work. Here are some potential reasons:

- *Wasn't newsworthy.* Perhaps your press release didn't have national appeal. Maybe it meant something to you but nothing to others. Next time, make sure your press release is meaningful enough to be used.

- *Was too long.* Maybe your press release took up too much space. It may have been considered for placement, but simply wouldn't fit in the space allowed. Next time, keep your release short—no longer than one page.

- *Had too many typos and grammatical errors.* Newspapers prefer to copy and paste your press release into their format without having to edit it. If your press release is poorly written so that it requires too much editing, it's easier for them to just find another press release. Next time, use spell check.

- *Not enough consistency.* Like anything else, the human brain responds to consistency and branding. If you send a press release out once a year, you're not building your brand among journalists and bloggers. Try sending a release out every one to two months, and they'll be more likely to recognize you or your company.

· ▣ · ▣ · ▣ ·

BOOKING BLACK RADIO INTERVIEWS

There are more than 400 radio stations across the country that have a combined listening audience of more than 18 million African Americans. About 75 percent of these stations have daily or weekly news and talk-radio programs that interview columnists, experts, and gurus on various topics.

Obviously, being interviewed on the radio is a very effective way to promote your company, your book, your organization, your website, etc. So how do you get invited to be on the air? Here are three proven strategies:

1. *Regularly send out relevant press releases.* News programmers and disc jockeys receive and read press releases all the time. The more you appear in the headlines, the more likely it is they'll invite you on the show. Remember to send out relevant and meaningful releases that will not only interest them but also fit their format. If possible, do this at least once a month.

2. *Write and distribute columns.* Write and distribute intelligently written columns or editorials on a weekly or biweekly basis. This shows that you're an expert on specific topics, and that you have helpful insight to share. Even more, it shows that you're professional and available to talk on the air.

3. *Send out a media advisory.* A media advisory is a brief note to the media informing them that you're available to discuss certain topics. For instance, if it's National Diabetes Week and you're an expert on the topic, you can distribute a formatted note to the press announcing that you're available for interviews to discuss your organization or general tips for diabetics. For the correct format of a media advisory, search online for "media advisory template."

Applying these three strategies when using online press release distribution services should help you produce the results you want.

• ▣ • ▣ • ▣ •

THE POWER OF PR: SWINE FLU VS. HIV/AIDS

The media are very, very powerful. It happens nearly every year that they report on some new development, blow it completely out of proportion and hundreds of millions of people feed into it. Consider the media's heavily publicized messages on swine flu in 2009. The outbreak supposedly began in Mexico. After the media announced the pandemic, people started talking about it, twittering about it, canceling their vacations, and even shooting their Mexican friends anxious looks. Few, however, bothered to understand the level of media hype. Consider this: in July 2009, the World Health Organization (WHO) stated that 700 people have died from the swine flu virus worldwide since H1N1 emerged in April. Compare this statistic to the November 2009 WHO report that an estimated 33.4 million people worldwide are living with HIV/AIDS. Which illness poses a greater threat to global public health? Shouldn't the uproar be about HIV/AIDS? The power of the media rests in its ability to shape peoples' opinions and influence what folks spend their precious time thinking about.

Entrepreneurs need to recognize these types of imbalances and use it to their advantage. You've now seen first-hand how the media can draw a huge amount of attention to any topic. Swine flu isn't the first health doomsday scenario floated before a nervous public. Remember West Nile virus, Mad Cow disease, anthrax, etc? All of these diseases have the potential to produce health epidemics—but people became aware of them because of the depth of media saturation.

Find a way to get the media to focus on your company. Find a way to get people talking about you and highlighting the unique contribution that your business makes. Create a relevancy buzz. Outline why your peers and/or supporters believe that you're the next big thing. Distribute press releases monthly, write and distribute original feature articles pertaining to your industry, etc. Consider staging an unforgettable publicity event. Write a book with a controversial title. Publicly challenge a major company or organization.

Never hesitate to give the media something newsworthy to talk about. The news industry thrives on topical new items. Be creative. Look for opportunities to jump on. Be bold and edgy, and most importantly—think big.

Consider this: If your business got just 1 percent of the media attention that focused on swine flu, how huge would that be?

• ▣ • ▣ • ▣ •

LEARN TO SPEAK LIKE OBAMA

Of the countless books that have been published since the 44th president's campaign, inauguration, and tenure as the newest leader of the free world, few have seized my entrepreneurial imagination like Shelly Leanne's *Say It Like Obama: The Power of Speaking with Purpose and Vision.*

This book is all about the power of persuasion, the art of presentation, and the most effective communication techniques. From building strong arguments and facing tough issues to inspiring a team or workforce to new levels of innovation and productivity, *Say It Like Obama* provides the tools necessary to instill positive change at every level of your organization by learning how to:

- Make a strong first impression

- Use body language and voice

- Establish common ground

- Gain trust and confidence

- Win hearts and minds

- Drive your points home

- Convey your vision through imagery and words that resonate

- Build to a crescendo and leave a lasting impression

Whether you're an entrepreneur with ambitions as a public speaker, a seasoned business owner, or community leader, *Say It*

Like Obama will provide you with presentation techniques that have inspired and mobilized audiences of every size. In the 21st century, it's never been clearer that there's great benefit in learning how to be an extraordinary communicator and to speak like our president.

Public Relations—Business Secrets

1. Submit press releases and columns at least once a month to get publicity for your company. BlackPR. com—an extensive press release distribution service to all black newspapers, magazines, TV and radio stations—services more than 1,000 news outlets.

2. Submit a press release through Free-Press-Release.com. It's actually free, but of course, it has upgrade options.

3. PRlog.org is another free press release distribution and submission service to consider.

4. Also look at PRleap.com for press release distribution. Doing so can help your search-engine optimization.

5. PRnewswire.com is an extensive press release distribution service to all national and international media outlets, but it is very expensive. A much more affordable alternative is MarketWire.com.

6. Send out a newsworthy press release at least once a month. Staying in front of the media will give your company a constant buzz, and the bigger media outlets will eventually start to notice you.

7. Write your press release as if you are writing an article. Write it in third-person format. This means you refer to yourself as "he" or 'she," and you refer to your company as "it." Never write a press release in first-person format, using "I" or "we" unless you're quoting yourself.

8. Give your press release or column a meaningful but relatively short title. Using a long title can be a huge mistake. If you absolutely feel your title must be long, try and break it up by using a subtitle.

9. Keep your press release to no more than one page. A longer release is too lengthy and looks very unprofessional.

10. Include a professional photo with your press release. Pictures speak a thousand words and can often enhance the effectiveness of your release. Make sure the photo is actually related to the content.

11. Writing a book is a great way to get free publicity. You can easily self-publish using services like Lulu.com or AuthorHouse.com. Be sure to have a clever title, and don't worry too much about making money from selling books. The publicity alone will be worthwhile.

12. List your profile on BlackExperts.com and BlackSpeakers.com—it's a great way to make yourself available for paid speaking engagements and primetime media interviews.

13. List yourself on Experts.com to make yourself available for speaking engagements and other promotional opportunities.

14. Launch a postcard marketing campaign. In my opinion, this is the most effective marketing method. Believe it or not, people respond to junk mail. I recommend that you use services like ModernPostcard.com or 48HourPrint.com to help you with the printing and mailing. The pricing is very reasonable.

15. From time to time, write and distribute a column voicing your opinion about a current issue pertaining to your industry. Columns, unlike press releases, can be written in first person using "I" or "we."

16. If you want to invite the media to an event, send out a media advisory—a brief announcement that includes instructions on how to apply for a press pass.

Authors—Business Secrets

1. Make sure your book has a title that really stands out. The more controversial, the better. Ninety percent of the people to whom you promote your book will never even read it, but the title alone can get their attention and make them buy.

2. Make sure your book cover is professionally designed. If you're not a graphic designer, don't try to do it on your own. Second to the book's title, your cover design is the most important part of your book.

3. Having a book signing is a great idea, but don't do it just to sign books. Make it a public spectacle so that you can benefit from the publicity. Give away free gifts if possible, and give a brief informative presentation related to the topic of your book. Do more than just read excerpts.

4. Endorsements by well-known celebrities, industry, or thought leaders. Get people to endorse your book, and feature their quotes on the back of the book. Many people will do this if you ask because it also means exposure for them.

5. Try and get as many radio interviews as possible. This can be done fairly easily by writing and distributing columns about a current issue related to the topic of your book.

6. Speak at local libraries. Not only will you be able to gain attention from people who like to read, but the library may actually purchase copies of your book.

7. Speak at local colleges. Many colleges welcome this, and may even start selling your book at their on-campus bookstore.

8. List your profile on BlackExperts.com and BlackSpeakers.com to make yourself available for speaking engagements and media interviews. Such exposure will help you promote your book before large audiences.

9. Promote your book at the annual National Black Book Festival, one of the largest black author events in the south. It's usually held in Houston, Texas. For more details, visit www.NationalBlackBookFestival.com.

10. Promote your book at the annual African American Publishers' Pavilion, a black authors' exposition held in partnership with Book Expo America. For more details, visit www.AmberBooks.com.

11. Promote your book at the annual Black Writers on Tour conference, one of the largest black author events on the west coast. It's usually held in Los Angeles, California. For more details, visit www. BlackWritersOnTour.com.

12. Promote your book at the annual Harlem Book Fair, an outdoor event for black authors and readers held in Harlem, New York. For more details, visit www.QBR.com.

13. Join BlackAuthorsConnect.com, a free online community of black authors who network and share resources.

14. Join BlackAuthorShowcase.com, a cooperative learning, teaching, and supporting community for black authors.

15. Consider advertising on AALBC.com, a very popular website for black book reviews and interviews.

16. Shoot a low-budget but high-quality book trailer about your book and post it online via YouTube. Then you can use the embed code to plug your video into all your social media profiles, and even onto your own website.

17. Find a topic on Wikipedia.com that's relevant to your book, and list your book's website as a resource. Yes, anyone can edit a Wikipedia page.

18. Consider using BookCrossing.com, an online tool that gives you a way to share your books. The concept is to randomly leave a book somewhere where someone might pick it up, and then track the book's journey as it's passed around the world.

19. Always give a free copy of your book to influential people. They're the ones who are most likely to pass it along to other influential people.

20. Read *How to Succeed in the Publishing Game* by Vickie Stringer. She is a best-selling author and the queen of hip-hop literature. This advice is especially relevant for urban fiction writers.

21. John Kremer, a book industry expert, offers great tips and resources for authors via his website www. BookMarket.com.

Public Speaking—Business Secrets

1. Join Toastmasters International, an organization that helps its members improve their communication and leadership skills while fostering self-confidence and personal growth. For more details, visit www. toastmasters.org.

2. Watch the pros. One great way to become a good speaker is to observe the styles and habits of great speakers. Learn from them and reinvent the wheel.

3. Dress professionally and comfortably. The better you look and feel, the easier it will be to give your speech.

4. If possible, become familiar with your environment before you speak. The more familiar you are, the more comfortable you'll be.

5. Know your material. If you're thoroughly prepared, you probably won't be too nervous. Know your topics, and don't try to wing it—even if you've given speeches before.

6. Make eye contact. You can refer to your notes but shouldn't be reading them word-for-word. Your eyes should connect with others in the audience.

7. Use hand gestures. Use your hands to express the points being made. Don't overdo it though, as this can also be a distraction to what you're saying.

8. Know your audience. Based on whom you're talking to, your speech should be adjusted to fit your audience. Obviously, your speech would sound different if you're talking to students as opposed to a room full of corporate executives.

9. Try to relax. It's normal to be a little nervous while speaking, but if it's obvious that you're nervous, you can appear amateurish. Convince others that you've done this a thousand times.

10. Control your speed. Never race through a speech. Take your time, and speak slightly slower than usual. Remember especially to pause on important points.

11. Ask rhetorical questions. Asking such questions is a great way to engage your audience, and encourages them to continue paying attention.

12. Be funny. Try to have a sense of humor. All audiences like to be humored. However, be careful not to use too many jokes. Even worse, don't use any corny jokes.

13. Keep it short. Unless people are expecting you to speak for an hour, try to keep your speech brief. Adults, like children, have attention spans, and many don't last very long. Always leave them wanting more.

14. Be yourself and act normal. People will be able to tell if you're pretending to be someone you're not. Your audience wants to hear from the "real" you—not some actor or actress.

CHAPTER 14

THE CYBERPRENEUR

THE BUSINESS OF TECHNOLOGY

As a contemporary entrepreneur it's impossible to stay competitive in business without accessing the internet to gather information, reach customers, or spot the latest trends. The same technology once used for entertainment or shopping can now help improve and expand your business—all with the click of a mouse.

The internet explosion has made start-ups for the ambitious entrepreneur a low- or nearly no-cost enterprise. All it takes is basic computer skills, access to a good PC or Mac, internet access, and a few essential peripherals, like an all-in-one scanner, printer, and fax machine, and a commitment to stay in the cyberworld saddle. Even if you operate a brick-and-mortar office space, chances are you still rely on technology. According to the SBA, "...today's very competitive business climate demands that business owners understand and use advanced technologies...it can help a business improve efficiencies and even expand operations."

As a virtual entrepreneur, your success in business can be greatly enhanced by your knowledge of and access to basic software programs, such as MS Word, Excel, or Power Point. Such tools put the miracle of advanced technology and communication at your fingertips. *Cyberpreneuring isn't the future—it's right now.*

• ▣ • ▣ • ▣ •

GET CONNECTED IN CYBERSPACE

The internet is a significant business leveler that can allow anyone with an entrepreneurial mindset to compete with the giants on the global playing field. Black entrepreneurs and businesses face the usual barriers to success including lack of access to capital and liquidity constraints cited by Robert W. Fairlie and Alicia M. Robb in their report: *Race and Entrepreneurial Success: Black, Asian, and White-Owned Businesses in the United States.* For me, the work of these scholars underscores that while minority entrepreneurs still face business survival challenges—now is not the time to put our heads in the sand. Consider these facts: Forrester Research, Inc., an independent technology and market research company, estimates that 47.3 million North American households have online access and of that number, about 55 percent of black households have internet access. In the six months prior to July 15, 2010, 95 percent of those households made online purchases.

"Time-starved consumers are becoming more comfortable using credit and bank cards to make purchases from security-backed virtual retailers," says the SBA. "And as these electronic consumers continue to purchase via this medium, e-commerce will become even stronger." So, if you haven't been conducting business online, it's time to make the commitment to explore the potential of conducting at least part of your business on the information superhighway—you could be missing out.

Gareth Knight's July 2010 article for memeburn.com on the emerging capabilities of the African continent for broadband service was particularly inspiring to me. "...international submarine communication cables are starting to ring the continent, bringing with them the promise of cheaper broadband. That means Africa will soon have the infrastructure to be able to compete more effectively in the online space than it did in the past. But Africa has missed out on several years of important learning in this space and now is the perfect time for African entrepreneurs to embrace business and technical expertise from the rest of the world and close that gap."

If you're like me you can see that this technological development can be a cyber-savvy entrepreneur's dream—a new market poised for rapid expansion in a whole new way. It's waiting for *you!*

• ▣ • ▣ • ▣ •

WEBSITE DESIGN STRATEGIES

When I encountered a new e-commerce resource in an unexpected solicitation from InternetRetailer.com, I was not only persuaded to attend their yearly conference, I became a customer. It completely revived my online presence.

Here was InternetRetailer.com's irresistible pitch: "You may think your web store looks just great and you have a right to be proud of it. But did you ever sit with a focus group to see what problems they had with it? Did you ever have top website designers analyze it to find flaws? And have you listened to e-retailers tell you how they've vastly improved online sales and conversion rates just by making basic design changes that eliminated the most common website design faux pas?"

This caught my attention, but what really made me a believer was InternetRetailer.com's web design wisdom, including:

- *The home page syndrome.* You put most of your design resources on the home page and treat product pages as mere information pages—not marketing opportunities.

- *Do it now—ask questions later.* You make a relatively minor change to your design without rigorously testing it. The next thing you know, your online sales are dropping.

- *It's just a store.* You think websites are just like stores and need only products neatly arranged. You forget that non-product content is often what attracts people to a site.

- *What are you—anti-social?* If your site doesn't use forums, blogs, and reviews, it fails to connect to the community it serves.

InternetRetailer.com is a great resource for the cyberpreneur. It provides a wealth of invaluable information to online merchants. Give yourself the leg up on your competitors and make time to consult with the experts on how to improve your website and your bottom line.

• ▣ • ▣ • ▣ •

DOES YOUR WEBSITE SELL?

Online retailers did more than $156 billion dollars in sales in 2009. Even in the face of the economic downturn, as companies continue to struggle, online sales continue to grow. Estimates forecast over $250 billion in online retail sales in 2010. Companies like eBay, Wal-Mart, and Best Buy generate millions in daily sales from their online business alone. Helen Leggatt of BizReport.com confirms that "Consumers are turning to the internet for all their shopping needs as it provides a better environment to price-check, ensuring the best bargains at a time when money is tight, along with the convenience and cost-saving elements of being able to shop from home."

Ramon Ray, journalist, technology evangelist, and editor of Smallbiztechnology.com, says that your website should be your best salesperson. He encourages entrepreneurs to transform their website into a sales representative. "If you think of your website as a salesperson, you'll begin to think of it as more than just a glorified brochure. You'll even want it to be better designed, since you probably want your sales reps to look good," Ray says.

Here are some good questions to ask yourself:

- Does your website know everything about your business that it should?

- Does your website have all your current products, services, and pricing?

- Do you measure your website's success (daily, weekly, monthly, quarterly, or annually)?

- On your website, do you offer "training" on your business fundamentals, new trends, or economic changes in your local market, or in the national business climate for your industry?

Ray adds, "Remember, your website is probably one of your best—if not the best—sales assets you have. If nurtured and taken care of, it will boost your sales and grow your business, just like a human salesperson."

• ▣ • ▣ • ▣ •

GIVE YOUR WEBSITE A MAKEOVER

If your website still looks like a template from 1995 or even 2005, you have a problem, my friend. Sadly, many black-owned businesses still have elementary-looking or outdated websites. Your website should be simple. However, there is a great difference between simplicity and looking unprofessional.

Point blank: Too many black websites still look unprofessional. The best way to determine whether or not yours needs some tweaking is to compare it to the leaders and trendsetters in your industry. For instance, if you sell cars, then you need to compare your website to the online industry leader, Cars.com. If you sell flowers, then you need to compare your website to 1800flowers. com, Teleflora.com or the newest national competitor Proflowers. com. Once you accept the fact that your website needs a redesign, here are some basic tips:

- *Keep the design simple.* Your site does not have to be intricate with a lot of details. Simplicity is always a winner.

- *Feature only two to three colors.* Develop a consistent color scheme and stick to it.

- *Don't overdo the multimedia.* Don't use animated images, unnecessary music and sounds, and unrelated videos. (Stay away from Java applets.)

- *Summarize your text, if possible.* Just because you have the space doesn't mean that you have to fill it up.

- *Be honest with yourself.* If you're not an experienced web professional, hire someone who is. Shop around, do your due diligence, and get busy.

• ▣ • ▣ • ▣ •

SHOULD YOUR WEBSITE USE FLASH?

Flash is a software application owned by Adobe Systems, the same company that produces Photoshop and Dreamweaver. Flash allows you to add animation and interactivity to your website. It's commonly used to display interactive pull-down menus, interactive advertisements, interactive videos, and even interactive video games. Flash represents consumers' increased demand for interactivity and innovation on the web.

Despite its useful and creative functionality, Flash is controversial among many web designers and developers.

I offer three Flash cautions for small business owners:

1. *Slow loading time.* Flash can slow down the loading time of your web pages. If your website is designed entirely using Flash, people may have to wait up to 30 seconds or more until the loading completes. Instead

of waiting around for your pages to load, a visitor is very likely to leave your website and find another one. Even if your website uses Flash moderately, it can still cause a loading delay.

2. *Not search-engine friendly.* Flash can make your website look and feel more interactive, but it can also make your website invisible to search-engines, because search-engine algorithms are written to crawl images and text, not flash applications. Experiment for yourself and conduct a search with any key word on Google or Yahoo. See how many of the top ten website rankings use Flash.

3. *Not mobile friendly.* More and more people are using their cell phones or smart phones to access the web, and guess what? Flash-based websites do not display correctly when accessed from a mobile device. If your entire website was built using Flash, it will not display at all.

   Apple, which has the fastest-growing market share for mobile devices, has purposely excluded support for Flash websites from the iPhone and iPad. Instead, Apple is endorsing an up-and-coming competitor called HTML5.

Undoubtedly, Flash has its place for websites that allow users to watch videos and play video games. However, for most small businesses dependent on search-engine traffic, I would suggest exploring other search-engine friendly options to produce the level of interactivity you're looking for.

● ▣ ● ▣ ● ▣ ●

ÜBER-TECH—SEARCH-ENGINE OPTIMIZATION

Search-engine optimization, or SEO, may sound super-technical. In reality, it refers to a great way to direct tons of traffic to your website.

Once you've developed meaningful original content, you're ready for increased online traffic. Companies pay anywhere from hundreds to millions of dollars each year for pay-per-click advertising, but if you're attracting traffic from the search-engines naturally—it's free.

Here are 10 elements that must be actively incorporated into your website to generate free traffic:

1. *Title tags.* Label each page title with what that specific page talks about.

2. *Meta key words.* Choose the top 10 key words describing your business.

3. *Meta descriptions.* Write attractive sentences that make people want more.

4. *Alternative texts.* Commonly overlooked—label your pictures with text.

5. *Inbound links.* Links from related and credible sites pointing to you.

6. *Anchor texts.* Should contain your top key word: ex. Business Coach.

7. *Generic domain.* If you sell cars, register www.buyacar.com, for instance.

8. *Sitemap.* Search-engines use this as a guide to all pages on your site.

9. *External linking.* Limit outgoing links from your site to 20.

10. *Key word ranking.* See how you rank for each term weekly.

SEO is complex and time-consuming stuff. So, if you don't have much experience with web development and marketing (and are actually generating traffic), hire an expert to help. The affordable SEO Experts are ranked on the first page of each search-engine for the term "SEO Expert" and they've been featured in

Entrepreneur magazine. Their expertise is definitely worth the investment. In this economy, free traffic is definitely the best traffic.

• ▣ • ▣ • ▣ •

WHY MOST BLACK WEBSITES DON'T GET REAL TRAFFIC

People ask me all the time why they can't increase customer traffic to their websites. Here's my answer: Because you don't spend the money, energy, and time necessary to produce the desired results. Too often, people believe that passing out flyers and business cards that list your website address is enough. What they fail to realize is that's the easy route that yields no results. If you want results, you have to take the hard, tedious, invest-your-money route. Most importantly, you must learn to be consistent and patient. You can't plant seeds one night and expect to pick flowers 24 hours later.

Here are two essential suggestions for increasing web traffic:

- *Invest in pay-per-click advertising.* Millions of businesses use this method to increase their web traffic. It's costly, but it can also be affordable. My favorite pay-per-click service is Google Adwords. However, there are several out there, including Yahoo Search Marketing, Adbrite.com, and the newest contenders— Facebook Ads and MySpace Ads.

   The concept of pay-per-click advertising is simple. You bid on key word search terms, and decide how much you want to pay whenever someone clicks on your ad. Typically, the rate is anywhere from $.10 to $.50 per click, but it can go much, much higher for certain key words. This method has resulted in great traffic-building results for my website network. Take my word for it—it works!

- *Learn the ropes of content marketing.* You and your website should be a go-to resource to industry professionals. The best way to establish yourself as a resource is to supply original and informative content. Host free seminars, write and distribute columns and articles to online media, create an e-book. These are a few ways to build your content muscles.

Mainstream newswire services, like PRWeb.com and PRLeap.com, and African American newswire services, like BlackPR.com, are excellent tools to help you get the word out on your latest newsworthy contributions. When writing your article, always remember to include your website address in your tagline. This will help readers access your site easily and increase your search-engine ranking. Your fresh, content-rich site will be more likely to come up first when people search for related key words. Make a commitment to write and distribute new content on a bi-weekly or monthly basis.

Although the process of building web traffic can be time-consuming and demanding, remember that if you invest the time and effort, the rewards can be amazing.

• ▣ • ▣ • ▣ •

Traffic Boosters—Let the Buyer Beware

"Boost Your Traffic Fast." "Get 10,000 visitors for $49." "Triple your traffic in 24 hours." These are some of the seductive ploys that these website-traffic-boosting services use to promote their services. Anytime you hear a claim like these, stay away—99 percent of these outfits are fraudulent. Such companies typically prey on gullible, inexperienced entrepreneurs. They also prey on minority businesses with newly established websites, recognizing that they're anxious to get more traffic.

Too often, such services don't send you traffic at all. If they do, it may be completely untargeted. You could wind up with 10,000 visitors who live in China visiting your website—because they've been tricked.

If you want to utilize a legitimate traffic boosting service, my personal recommendation is to stick with Google Adwords, Yahoo Search Marketing, Microsoft Ad Center, Facebook Ads, MySpace Ads, and Adbrite.com.

• ▣ • ▣ • ▣ •

STOP SAYING "HITS"

Nobody cares how many *hits* your website gets. Nowadays, it's all about how many monthly unique visitors you can verify. Consider the following touchstones from a recent article on WebMarketingNow.com:

"A 'hit' is not a visitor to the website but a hit on the web server. A hit on the web server can be a graphic, java applet, HTML file, etc. So, if a site has 79 small graphics on the page, every visitor to the site registers as 80 hits on the server (79 graphics plus the HTML file). In this case, 80,000 hits translates to just 1,000 visitors."

Now ask yourself this: If I were interested in someone else's web traffic, would I be interested in their "hits" or their actual unique visitors? From now on, stop using counters to measure your web traffic—because these only measure page views. Use a web traffic-analysis program, such as Google Analytics, that will give you the number of actual visitors and other vital information, such as where visitors are coming from, what paths your visitors are taking, and which pages are the main exit points of your site.

Occasionally, some advertisers may be interested in how many page views your website can generate. This is because they want to know how many times their banner ads will be displayed, even if they're displayed more than once to the same person. This is much different from a "hit"—which to those in the know means absolutely nothing.

• ▣ • ▣ • ▣ •

EVERY BLACK-OWNED BUSINESS SHOULD BE USING GOOGLE

Google is the most innovative and helpful technology company of the early 21st century. Yes, more innovative than Microsoft, Yahoo and eBay. Why? Google helps small businesses prevail. Google Adsense helps small websites make money by matching ads to your site's content and earning you money whenever your visitors click on them. Google Adwords helps small businesses effectively market themselves by advertising to people searching on Google and its advertising network, advertising to an audience that's already interested in you.

My company utilizes Google every single day to get leads and sales, and generate more revenue. We've been Google customers for many years now, and plan to stick with the proven innovator for the long haul.

• ▣ • ▣ • ▣ •

"ADD THIS" TO YOUR WEBSITE TO SHARE CONTENT

There's a new free tool that every savvy entrepreneur should add to his or her website. It's called "Add This" and it helps website publishers and bloggers spread their content across the web by allowing visitors to bookmark and share content to their favorite social media destinations. Now visitors to your website can easily share your content with their friends and followers on Facebook, Twitter, MySpace, and other popular social media sites. They can also easily share content via e-mail. Not only is this download easy to install, it offers sophisticated analytics to help you understand how and where your content is being shared. For more details, visit AddThis.com.

• ▣ • ▣ • ▣ •

WHAT IS RSS?

You've likely heard the term RSS. It's an acronym for Really Simple Syndication. All it means is that you can subscribe free to content from various websites and blogs, and have it delivered to a single page—commonly known as an RSS reader.

In light of the seemingly infinite amount of information available on the web, this service is very helpful. For instance, suppose you regularly frequent WashingtonPost.com, BusinessWeek.com, WSJ.com, BlackEnterprise.com, and other news sites. Instead of visiting each website every day, you can create your own customized home page to see the stories (or feeds) all at once.

My favorite RSS reader is iGoogle (google.com/ig) because it's very simple and fast to use. Google has another one called Google Reader (google.com/reader), which is a little more sophisticated.

Using RSS benefits entrepreneurs because it enables you to better keep up with your business publications. It can be overwhelming to frequent five to ten different news websites every day. RSS is the solution, and it even helps you better identify the articles that appeal most to you.

To subscribe to an RSS feed, simply scan your favorite website for a link that says "Subscribe Via RSS" or look for the commonly used orange logo. Many cell phones, such as the BlackBerry or iPhone, have mobile applications that also enable you to subscribe to and access RSS feeds. The actual mobile application may have a fee, but subscribing to the feed itself will always be free.

• ▣ • ▣ • ▣ •

THE POWER OF ONLINE TESTIMONIALS AND REFERENCES

Every entrepreneur should have an understanding of the power of business testimonials, and client and customer references. They are simply personal endorsements and can make a huge difference to your company's bottom line.

People are extremely skeptical about doing business with unknown companies—especially if your business is strictly online. Something as simple as a good experience testimony can give potential customers the confidence needed to buy whatever you're selling.

Here's how to maximize positive endorsements:

- Take your best five to ten clients and put their contact info on a list that you can easily e-mail to those who are interested. Be sure to let your clients know that, from time to time, you may have someone contact them. Most clients don't usually mind this—as long as people don't call them every single week.

- In addition, post some selling testimonials on your website. Use graphics or customer photos where ever you can. Check out my website: BlackExperts.com/testimonials.html.

Adding this one element to your website can dramatically increase your chances of converting a potential client into an actual client. The power of word-of-mouth advertising and what satisfied customers have to say can be very influential on potential customers.

On the flip side, be cautious when contemplating doing business with an unfamiliar company. Search its website for testimonials. If there are none, call the company and ask for a list of references. This way you can talk to their actual clients, who can confirm whether or not the company's legit.

The absence of testimonials or references on a website may be a sign that the company is a start-up venture or that someone's running a scam. In any event, never let your customer click away from your products or services because you lack credible and verifiable performance feedback.

• ▣ • ▣ • ▣ •

How Social Networking Can Help Your Business

Social networking is linking people together to create online communities. They're used by millions of individuals—and increasingly businesses—as a platform for daily connection and interaction.

At one point I thought it was something only college students could benefit from. Now, like many business brokers, I know otherwise. Thanks to websites like LinkedIn.com, entrepreneurs can benefit greatly from professional social networking that can indeed help grow your business.

Social networking can increase:

- *Visibility.* Post a public profile about your current professional status and professional background. This enables others to see who you are and what your accomplishments are, and encourages them to connect with you for business.

- *Targeting.* Discover potential business partners and clients with similar interests. Once identified, you can add them to your network for others to see whom you're affiliated with.

- *Endorsement.* People who know you (or who have done business with you) can post their recommendations about you. Such endorsements are good for others to see when considering whether or not to connect with you.

- *Confirmation.* Social networking enhances your search-engine results whenever someone "googles" you. This will validate you when people are conducting research to confirm if you are who you claim to be.

- *Virtual connection.* Link directly new business contacts entirely from your computer. While nothing can replace face-to-face communication at conferences, in our time-crunched world, connecting with people in the comfort of your own home or office is a very important opportunity.

• ▣ • ▣ • ▣ •

TWEET! TWEET!

If you don't know what a "tweet" is, you are officially behind the curve. But don't panic—read on and you'll be back on track in no time. Twitter is an online tool that allows you to communicate and stay connected with friends, family, and colleagues. Yes, I know what you're thinking: You can already do this through social networking and blogging.

Twitter, often referred to as micro-blogging, distills communication into one or two short sentences—maximum 140-character transmissions. Twitter allows people to follow you and you to follow them. In this context, follow means "to keep up with what other people are doing" or "to stay in the know."

In January 2010, 73.5 million unique visitors logged on to Twitter and over 1.2 billion tweets were transmitted. Millions use Twitter every day. Some use it for pointless, self-indulgent banter. Others use it to create meaningful dialogue and share content. I've been seriously tweeting and have left my initial skepticism behind. Tweeting is definitely something that all entrepreneurs should seriously consider, If you don't already have a Twitter account, it's time to get one. It's 100 percent free. If you do have a Twitter account, it's time to start tweeting. For more details or to sign up, visit twitter.com. To follow me on Twitter, visit twitter.com/DanteLee.

• ▣ • ▣ • ▣ •

ARE YOU TWELLOWING AND TWEETBEEPING?

You've already subscribed to Twitter, right? Twitter's exponential growth makes it a very useful tool for getting and retaining new clients. It's also an amazing way to stay in the know. Check out two new sites that can enhance your Twitter experience. Twellow.com helps you easily find relevant people to follow on Twitter. Essentially, it's a Yellow Book directory for Twitter profiles and is much more extensive than the search feature on Twitter's website. I use this site all the time to find people who are connected to the businesses that I'm most interested in. For instance, if I search for relevant key words, such as "supplier diversity," "minority business," or "diversity recruiting," I find people and start following and interacting with them. Eventually, these are people who'll inquire about my services.

Another valuable site that entrepreneurs can benefit from is called TweetBeep.com. It allows you to get e-mail alerts whenever someone twitters about you or your company. You can also specify other key words that may be of interest to you.

• ▣ • ▣ • ▣ •

TOP 10 TWITTER ACCOUNTS FOR MINORITY ENTREPRENEURS

Twitter is a great way to connect with people and share valuable information, especially since you can tweet through most mobile devices. Those who actively tweet have found great benefits. Like all technology, Twitter can either be an invaluable tool or a total time waster. To make Twitter a bona fide entrepreneurial asset, I recommend that all minority entrepreneurs follow these top 10 Twitter accounts:

1. *@BlackEnterprise* is the official account for *Black Enterprise* magazine, the largest publication for African American business professionals and entrepreneurs.

2. *@BizGrants* is the official account for the National Institute of Business Grants, a leading resource for business funding opportunities.

3. *@MBNUSA* is the official account for Minority Business News USA (MBN USA), an award-winning magazine that's an authority on supplier and workforce diversity.

4. *@MiBizNet* is the official account for the Minority Business Network, an organization that actively promotes the competitiveness and growth of minority businesses.

5. *@NASEtweets* is the official account for the National Association of the Self-Employed (NASE), a nonprofit, nonpartisan organization that provides resources to entrepreneurs and micro-businesses.

6. *@EntMagazine* is the official account for *Entrepreneur* magazine, the premier magazine of the small-business community.

7. *@WSJ* is the official account for *The Wall Street Journal*, one of the world's leading resources for daily financial news.

8. *@ExecTweets* is the official account powered by Microsoft that helps you find and follow the top business executives on Twitter.

9. *@SmallBusinessAd* is the official account for the federal Small Business Administration (SBA), offering the latest news and tips to help your business succeed.

10. *@SmallBusiness* is the official account for SmallBusiness.com, an online resource for news and advice pertaining to small businesses.

• ▣ • ▣ • ▣ •

DID YOU GET YOUR FACEBOOK USERNAME?

Originally, I was not a big fan of using Facebook for business purposes, but the evolution of Facebook as a business tool has benefited a lot of entrepreneurs and established some impressive track records. Today, Facebook offers a variety of business-friendly options, such as Facebook Pages, Groups, Advertising, Polls, and Applications, all capable of supporting the activities relevant to the creative business person or entrepreneur.

You can also employ a new feature that allows you to personalize your Facebook URL (web address) by selecting a unique username. It will appear in the location bar of your browser after "http://www.facebook.com" when you view your profile. For instance, my personalized URL is www.Facebook.com/DanteLee.

Since so many people use Facebook, this is a really neat feature because it makes it very easy for people to find you. In addition, over time your page will start to show up in search-engine results whenever people "google" you. Don't procrastinate, though, because if someone takes the username you want, there's nothing you can do about it. If this happens, consider other options. For instance, I could have also registered Facebook.com/LeeDante or Facebook.com/Dante.Lee or even Facebook.com/DanteMLee. Whichever option you chose, just remember that you cannot change it later—so get it right the first time around.

Also, don't even think about name squatting—trying to capitalize on someone else's name. Facebook reserves the right to remove and reclaim any username at any time for any reason. To choose and activate your username, visit facebook.com/username.

● ▣ ● ▣ ● ▣ ●

CREATE YOUR OWN SOCIAL NETWORK

My business partner, Will Moss, has built a unique tool that allows people to create their own social network for free. It's called Connect Platform (connectplatform.com), and the same technology is used to power some of our sites, including HBCU-Connect.com, BlackHistory.com, BlackWomenConnect.com, and others.

The service is designed for individuals, businesses, groups, and that organizations want to create their own interactive online communities. The concept is perfect for celebrities, authors, speakers, etc. It also works very well for organizations like the NAACP or the Urban League, or even church groups and family reunions.

You may wonder why it's a good idea to create your own social network, when sites like Facebook and LinkedIn already exist. Here are five good reasons:

1. It's your own community. Creating your very own social network allows you to build your own online community. It's good to be part of other social networks, but it's also a plus to have one that is completely positioned around your brand.

2. It creates brand loyalty. Having your own social network will heavily engage your customers or supporters. Social networks are interactive and encourage people to visit your site more than just once.

3. You're in control. Having a page on Facebook is great, but you're not really in control. Creating your own social network allows you to control your content, add your logo, design your own look, and more.

4. It leaves an impression. If you create an online community with powerful resources and relevant people to interact with, people will be drawn to you and your brand, and more inclined to buy your products and services. Not only that, you'll be valued as the can-do person who brought everybody together.

5. It's free. Creating your own social network can be done within minutes, and it's 100 percent free. The only catch is that banner ads will appear on your site. For a modest fee, however, they can be removed.

For more details about how to create your own social network, visit www.connectplatform.com.

• ▣ • ▣ • ▣ •

DON'T JUST DOWNLOAD ANYTHING

If you want to really mess up your computer, keep downloading software from irreputable companies. In no time, your computer will be infested with harmful viruses, spyware, and adware programs. To be safe, always download your software from www. Download.com—a free directory containing just about all the available software published by reputable companies.

If you can't find it on their website, my suggestion is to ONLY download from the following companies: Microsoft, Yahoo, Google, Adobe, and Apple. It is also safe to download products (such as drivers and updates) directly from certain hardware companies, including Sony, Toshiba, Gateway, Compaq, HP, etc. The point is to be extremely cautious when downloading. If it seems suspicious, don't download it.

• ▣ • ▣ • ▣ •

AUTOMATICALLY BACK UP
YOUR COMPUTER WITH CARBONITE

I'm always surprised when I hear entrepreneurs say that their computer crashed and they lost everything. Put simply, you have to back up your computer regularly. If not, you could indeed lose everything—and there may not be any viable way to recover all the invaluable information you've created. One service that I've used and developed confidence in is Carbonite—it automatically backs up your files and stores them online. If you're like me and hate manually backing up to a CD, flash drive, or hard drive—this service is perfect.

What I like best about Carbonite is that you can access your files remotely, and the cost, $54.95 annually, is very reasonable. You can back up your entire computer no matter how many files you have. If you create a new file or edit an existing file, it too will automatically get backed up. In addition, Carbonite has an easy to install free iPhone app that allows you to see, open, and share your files right from your cell phone. You don't have to be a network administrator and you don't need a high level of technical skill. It's relatively easy.

I usually don't recommend products, but honestly—I can't resist. For entrepreneurs who lack an IT person or a help desk, I vote for the Carbonite backup.

• ▣ • ▣ • ▣ •

SKYPE FOR BUSINESS

Skype is a popular online tool that allows face-to-face connection with business colleagues through video conferencing anywhere in the world for free—right from your own personal computer. It's a very unique service and it works extremely well. The company, owned in part by eBay, generates revenue by charging for other features, such as call forwarding, text messaging, and Skype-to-Landline calls.

Although commonly used for personal connections with family and friends, Skype has recently released a dedicated business version. Essentially, it has the same features as the standard version but also includes Windows Installer (commonly known as MSI), which makes it easy to install Skype to multiple computers in your company. It also gives more control to IT administrators. Skype is a great resource for small businesses with employees operating from different locations.

• ▣ • ▣ • ▣ •

IPHONE VS. BLACKBERRY

I'll get right to the point: iPhone rules. Hands down. Before you react, please understand that I've owned both phones. I'm not just repeating what I've heard. I am speaking from first-hand experience. BlackBerry is like having an Atari (if you know what that is), and iPhone is like having a Playstation 3. BlackBerry is like having a Toyota, and iPhone is like having a Lamborghini. Black-Berry is like having a small black and white TV with three channels, and iPhone is like having a 60-inch flat screen HD plasma with 1,000 satellite channels.

In other words, BlackBerry is not my smart-phone of choice. Granted, at the end of 2009, iPhones had 30 million units sold compared to BlackBerry's 28.5 million, but with the advent of the latest iPhone 4G technology, even with the antenna problem, the estimates are that in the next 18 months iPhones will become the unqualified smart-phone market leader with a mind-boggling 100 million subscribers. No matter what the final tally is, what I can say for sure is this: If you try the iPhone, you'll never go back. And yes, it's well worth switching to the AT&T Wireless network. If your network doesn't work with the iPhone, hold on—industry insiders say help may be on the way.

Cyberpreneur—Business Secrets

TECHNOLOGY

1. Get an iPhone. In addition to this smart-phone's unique phone features, Apple reports that there are at least 225,000 third-party applications officially available on the App Store, with over 5 billion total downloads. There are no doubt hundreds of apps that can be very useful to your business.

2. Phase out your traditional phone services, and consider switching to a VOIP. These are internet phones that'll cost you a lot less in monthly bills and usually offer unlimited domestic and international

talk time. Check out consumer reviews on the most popular services from Vonage, Magic Jack, and Skype, and create your own tailor-made VOIP experience,.

3. Buy a business card scanner. It will automatically convert your business cards into an electronic directory on your computer. For more details, visit www.CardScan.com.

4. When browsing the internet, don't automatically assume that Internet Explorer is your only choice. Internet Explorer has a lot of security flaws. Use Mozilla Firefox instead. For more details, visit www. Firefox.com.

5. Before you invest the latest upgrade of Microsoft Office, consider using OpenOffice. It's an open-source office software suite for word processing, spreadsheets, presentations, graphics, databases, and more. It's very comparable to Microsoft Office, and it's available for free at www.OpenOffice.org

6. E-readers are the rage and the battle for your digital dollars is just starting to heat up. Whether you chose an iPad, Kindle, Sony Reader, or the Nook, you'll now have the opportunity to carry a small library with you wherever you go on a relatively small and lightweight portable device. E-readers are perfect for storing books and much more. May the best e-reader win!

INTERNET AND SOCIAL NETWORKING

1. Facebook.com began as a great tool to connect with family and friends, however today many entrepreneurs use Facebook to brand and build their business. Commit to keeping current with all of the

new business possibilities that Facebook can bring to your marketing efforts. Remember, this social networking tool is not just for college kids anymore.

2. Twitter.com one of the easiest social networking tools to get started with. Essentially, it allows you to micro-blog about what's up with you and your business to your followers. Millions of people use Twitter daily and it's an amazing way to promote your brand and your business. If you don't have an account, sign up today—it's free. If you do have an account, use it.

3. LinkedIn.com is a great way to connect with relevant professionals and colleagues. Create an account and actively use it to connect with others. The service is 100 percent free.

4. Business.com is a search-engine and directory for anything to do with business. Not only should you use it when looking for services, but you should also consider listing your business.

5. ConnectPlatform.com is a free online tool that allows African American individuals, groups, and organizations to create their very own online communities via a social network. Your members will be able to post blogs, photos, and videos, and interact with each other.

6. Ning.com, similar to ConnectPlatform, is another free social networking tool that allows you to create your own online community.

7. KeywordDiscovery.com is an online tool that helps you get an idea of how many times a specified key word is searched. This is helpful to know when you're launching a pay-per-click key word advertising campaign with any of the search-engines.

8. TrackVia.com allows you to manage your database online. This is helpful when you have several people adding, editing, and deleting information.

9. eFax.com is a very useful tool that allows you to receive faxes via your e-mail, and send faxes through your computer.

10. Instant messenger services are being increasingly used in business to communicate with clients, colleagues, and employees. The problem is that there are so many different ones: MSN Messenger, AOL Instant Messenger, Yahoo Messenger, ICQ, etc.—and they don't allow cross-communication. One service provider called Pidgin does allow you to communicate with anyone no matter what instant messenger service they're using. For more details, visit www.Pidgin.im.

11. SitePal.com is a unique service that allows you to add a human touch to your website. The company allows you to design a speaking animated character that can easily be added to your website or blog. You can program the character to look just like you and say anything you want.

12. AfricanAmericans.net is a free tool that allows you to network with thousands of black professionals.

13. BlackWomenConnect.com is a free online social network for professional African American women.

14. Sisterpreneurs.Ning.com is a free online social network for black women entrepreneurs.

15. Both iGoogle.com and Google.com/reader allow you to subscribe to RSS feeds. RSS stands for "Really Simple Syndication," which means that you can subscribe free to content from various websites and blogs, and have it

delivered to one single page—commonly known as an RSS reader.

16. HelloTxt.com allows you to simultaneously post status updates across multiple social networks and micro-blogs, including Facebook, LinkedIn, Plaxo, Ning, and Twitter.

17. DailyLit.com allows you to receive short book installments by e-mail or RSS feed. This is perfect for reading business books just a little bit each day.

18. Scribd.com is a social publishing site deemed the YouTube for document sharing. It provides a central storage place to publish and discuss original writing and documents.

19. Skrbl.com allows you to engage in online whiteboarding. You can write, draw, or just scribble your ideas. You can give out the URL of your Skrbl board and collaborate live with others, functioning as an online meeting space.

20. LinkPopularity.com is a tool that shows you which websites are linking to your website.

21. Box.net allows you to create an online workspace. You can share and access your spreadsheets, presentations, and other documents on the web.

22. Blogsvertise.com is a great platform that allows you to pay bloggers to blog about your product or services. This helps with web traffic and SEO links.

TWITTER TIPS

1. Don't start automating your tweets. This will only make you look impersonal and faceless. People are

following you on Twitter because they want to follow YOU, not some automated script. Avoid services like TwitterFeed.com that will automatically post your blog feeds. Do this yourself manually because not every blog post needs to be tweeted. Keep your tweets meaningful.

2. Be conversational. Don't just use Twitter to post a bunch of links. Talk in first person, and be you. After all, that's why people are following you in the first place.

3. Don't just follow anybody. Twitter is not about random interactions. You want to interact with people and brands that are relevant to you.

4. Ask questions. If you have a question pertaining to your industry, why not post it on Twitter? Many times, the people following you will have the answer and will reply very promptly.

5. Retweet other people's tweets. If it's newsworthy and it's relevant to your followers, retweet it. Not only will you get credit for sharing a resourceful tweet, but you'll also gain more followers.

6. Reply when people talk to you. Whether it's a public message or a direct message, always reply when someone communicates with you or mentions you. Remember that the more dialogue you engage in, the more followers you get.

7. Don't be a salesman. People on Twitter do not want to be bombarded with sales pitches. Be indirect. Just say resourceful things and eventually people will inquire about your products and services.

8. Use TweetLater.com—a tool that allows you to schedule your tweets for future dates.

9. Tweetie is an application for the iPhone that allows you to manage multiple Twitter accounts. Not only can you send tweets and retweets, but you can also follow and unfollow people right from your cell phone.

10. TweetDeck is an application for the iPhone, the BlackBerry, and other cell phones—that also allows you to manage your Twitter account.

WEBSITE TIPS

1. Remember that a website is only useful if people are actually going to it. Be sure to promote your website in everything you do. For instance, it should be on your business cards, in your e-mail signature, on your promotional material, on all your social network profiles, etc.

2. Stay away from animated gifs and Java applets. Shockingly, many business websites still have flashy cartoonish images and scripts. Not only does this look unprofessional, but it often makes your website act very sluggish.

3. Having your site designed in Flash may look nice, but people on mobile devices will see nothing when they visit your website. In addition, many libraries will disable Flash applications from running and/or will not update their computers to process the latest version. Never forget that Flash makes it difficult for search-engines to read the content of your site—which can result in a lower ranking.

4. Minimize the text on your website. Too often, business websites contain far too many words. You want to summarize as much as possible, and only mention the

important things that need to be said—who, what, why, when, and how.

5. Never have music playing on your website. This is unprofessional and makes your company look amateurish. The only exceptions are if you are a recording artist and/or if your company is a record label.

6. Always have current contact info and/or a contact form on your website. FormSpring.com is a great tool that can help you implement this.

7. Make sure that all of the pages on your website have meta tags for keywords and descriptions. This will help search-engines better index your website. If you don't know what meta tags are, you have no excuse. Google this term and educate yourself.

BUSINESS-BUILDING RESOURCES

CHAPTER 15

MENTORING AND EDUCATIONAL ORGANIZATIONS

1. The Small Business Administration is a key resource for any small business owner. It offers advisory services that include business planning, loan application, and certification help. Find out more at SBA.gov. Recently, Google and the Small Business Administration partnered to create a URL dedicated to small business needs, called Tools for Online Success. The site features tutorials, videos, and tips from small business people who have used the web to benefit their ventures. Topics range from analytics and search-engine optimization to how to incorporate these technological innovations into your business. Visit: http://www.google.com/help/sba.

2. The National Black Chamber of Commerce offers opportunities for education and networking. It is a nonprofit, nonpartisan, nonsectarian organization dedicated to the economic empowerment of African American communities. For more details, visit www.NationalBCC.org.

3. Intuit and the National Black Chamber of Commerce have combined to create "Small Business United."

Their offerings include free software, like QuickBooks; free website hosting and toll-free phone support seven days a week; six months' free payroll service; free incorporation services; free credit card processing; free retail management software; and more. To find out more, visit smallbusinessunited.com.

4. The Minority Business Development Agency, through the federal Commerce Dept., operates five regional business development centers that help minority entrepreneurs launch and boost their companies. In addition to tools and guidance, the centers help minority-owned businesses find financing. Find out more at mdba.gov.

5. IBM's Small & Medium Enterprise Toolkit offers online advice, mentoring, and tools for women and minority business owners. Find out more at us.smetoolkit.org/us/en.

6. NMSDC, WBENC, and the SBA's 8(a) program are the three main certifying agencies for minority and women business owners. The first two are primarily for corporate contracts, but they can also help you network with other women or minority business owners who have their own contracts to fill.

7. Count Me In offers peer mentoring and professional coaching to women business owners. Its marquee event, Make Mine a Million, is a yearlong online competition to build a business to $1 million in revenues. To find out more about this inspiring nonprofit, go to makemineamillion.org.

8. The National Association of Women Business Owners is the only dues-based organization representing the interests of all women entrepreneurs across all industries. It boasts over 7,000 members and

80 chapters across the country. With far-reaching clout and impact, NAWBO is a one-stop resource for propelling women business owners into greater economic, social, and political spheres of power worldwide. For more information go to http://www.nawbo.org.

9. The Women's Business Enterprise National Council (WBENC), founded in 1997, is the largest third-party certifier of businesses owned, controlled, and operated by women in the United States. WBENC, a national 501(c)(3) nonprofit, partners with 14 Regional Partner Organizations to provide its national standard of certification to women-owned businesses throughout the country. WBENC is also the nation's leading advocate of women-owned businesses as suppliers to America's corporations. For more information go to www.wbenc.org.

10. The National Women's Business Council, a policy advisory council to the president and Congress, serves as an information clearinghouse. Resources include research on entrepreneurship, papers on current issues that affect entrepreneurs, and lists of other organizations that may provide aid. To find out more information, go to www.nwbc.gov.

11. National Minority Supplier Development Council, Women's Business Enterprise National Council (WBENC), and the SBA's 8(a) program are the three main certifying agencies for minority and women business owners. The first two are primarily for corporate contracts, but they can also help you network with other women or minority business owners who have their own contracts to fill.

12. Business School Intensives. Many colleges and universities offer significant resources for entrepreneurs,

and plenty are open to the community. For established businesses, the Tuck School of Business at Dartmouth offers one-week courses, such as Building the High-Performing Minority Business, and Growing the Minority Business to Scale. Other schools have programs for launching or growing a business. Among Babson College's offerings is Moving from Managing to Leading, an executive course for women leaders. The Kellogg School of Management at Northwestern University also offers an executive program in partnership with the National Minority Supplier Development Council.

TRAVEL TIPS

1. If you really want to find the best deal fast, use www.Kayak.com or www.Sidestep.com. These sites are extremely powerful travel search-engines that will crawl every airline and travel agency's website (including Orbitz, Expedia, and Priceline) for the cheapest deal in about 15 seconds.

2. Subscribe to TravelZoo.com to get e-mail alerts about the best travel deals and specials. FareCast.com allows you to search for airplane tickets from all the major airlines, and find hotel rooms at all the major hotels. No big deal, right? It's their "Low Fare Prediction" that will predict whether or not the ticket prices shown will rise or drop that make them a worthwhile travel site.

3. BingTravel.com allows you to track fares and will tell you when and when not to buy a plane ticket for a route that you specify. Literally, they will say "Don't buy, fares will go down" or "Buy this ticket now, fares will go up."

4. Fly.com is an innovative travel search-engine that can help you find the best prices on flights from hundreds

of airlines and online travel agencies with just one quick and easy search.

5. Virgin America Airlines offers a power outlet and internet access at every seat. Not only can you connect to the internet, but you can keep your laptop or mobile device plugged in.

6. LastMinuteTravel.com provides the best last-minute pricing on airfare, hotels, rental cars, and more.

7. When it comes to getting travel deals, employ a multipronged approach. This ranges from constantly checking your favorite travel site to following these sites on Twitter and Facebook for constant updates (consider creating a Twitter travel list). Also subscribe to preferred website newsletters so you can track pricing trends to your favorite destinations and get the deals as soon as they're posted.

8. Wait, but not too long. While holding out can mean great deals, when it comes to airfare, there seems to be a point when airlines understand you are at the point of no return and thus start raising the prices. While this is not the case in all instances, experiment to see when it's time to book before the last-minute fare boomerang.

9. Beware of the 1 A.M. theory: A money-savvy colleague told me to check the airfares at about 1 A.M. since that's when airlines make price changes. But you can also lose out on a good deal booking around this time as well. In a matter of minutes fares for the same exact flight can increase exponentially.

10. Fly Southwest Airlines as much as possible. They don't charge you a fee if you need to change your flight itinerary, and they don't charge you to check bags.

Even more, its Rapid Rewards program is the easiest of all the airlines to earn a free flight.

11. Southwest Airlines allows you to earn points toward a free flight whenever you eat at a restaurant in its network. For more info, visit www. RapidRewardsDining.com. Southwest also allows you to earn points toward a free flight whenever you send someone flowers or a gift basket. For more info, visit http://rapidrewards.flowerclub.com.

12. You don't have to use a credit card to earn frequent flyer points anymore. Many banks now have debit cards that earn points too.

13. Use Hotels.com to find and compare the best hotel rates in the world. Many times, you can find a very good deal of up to 30 percent off by paying for your stay up front.

14. Use BedandBreakfast.com or BBonline.com to find bed and breakfast inns. Many business travelers prefer these types of lodging. The cost is usually reasonable, and the experience can be a very enjoyable change from traditional hotels.

15. When traveling for business, save yourself a lot of money by renting cars from Payless Car Rental. Its rates are generally a lot lower than major rental companies. The only drawback is that they do not offer rental services in every state. For more details, visit www.PaylessCarRental.com.

16. When traveling for business in California, Phoenix, Vegas, Seattle, Kansas City, Salt Lake City, and Miami—consider renting from Fox Rent-A-Car. They offer good rental cars at major discounts. For more info, visit www.FoxRentACar.com.

17. RentalCars.com allows you to compare rates of all the major rental car companies all at once.

PHONE APPS

1. *Kayak.* This app, modeled after the popular website Kayak.com, allows you to search many airlines and travel sites all at once. Right from your cell phone, you can easily determine the lowest airfare, hotel rates, and rental car rates. Cost: Free.

2. *Negotiator.* This app, released by Priceline.com, also allows you to search multiple sites for the lowest airfares, hotel rates, and rental car rates. In addition, right from your cell phone, you can negotiate for the rate that you want—often resulting in savings of up to 80 percent. Cost: Free.

3. *Southwest.* This app, from Southwest Airlines, is the only app that allows you to book and manage Southwest flights. You can also manage your points if you're a Rapid Rewards member. Cost: Free.

4. *Flight Track Pro.* This app helps you manage and organize your upcoming flights. It stores your confirmation numbers, allows you to view live flight maps, and will notify you in advance (via push notification) if your flight is delayed or canceled. Cost: $9.99.

5. *Trip It.* This app, from TripIt.com, is similar to Flight Track Pro, but also allows you to manage and organize your hotel and rental car reservations. It stores confirmation numbers and allows you to easily share your itinerary with friends and family. Cost: Free.

6. *iSwipe* is an application for the iPhone that allows you to securely process credit card numbers with address verification—right from your cell phone.

7. *SlyDial* is an application for the iPhone that allows you to place a call and skip right to the end user's voicemail; the phone never even rings. It only works if you are calling a person's cell phone number, but can be useful to leave a quick message for a client or colleague.

8. *ExecTweets* is an application for the iPhone that helps you find and follow the top business executives on Twitter.

9. *The New York Times* has an application on the BlackBerry and the iPhone that allows you to get their latest headlines with the full articles.

10. *The Wall Street Journal* has an application on the BlackBerry and the iPhone that allows you to get their latest news and commentary with the full articles. You can also watch video and listen to audio.

11. *HowCast* has an application on the iPhone that allows you to watch videos on how to do anything. The videos vary, but many are related to business and professional development.

12. *iProcrastinate* is an application on the iPhone that's consistently voted as the best app for time and project management.

13. *Bloomberg* has an application on the iPhone that allows you to get the latest news on the stock market and the economy. You get up to date reports on all the major markets—Dow Jones Industrial Average, NASDAQ, Nikkei, and many more—from all around the world.

14. *iXpenseIt* is an application for the iPhone that is a mobile expense recording solution. It's especially handy for keeping track of business expenses when you're traveling.

15. *Jott* is an application for the iPhone that allows you to record your million-dollar ideas or random thoughts when you speak. Within a minute or so, it will also transcribe your voice notes into text.

16. *WorldMate* is an application for the iPhone and BlackBerry that allows you to store and manage your flight itineraries, hotel stays, and rental car reservations.

17. *LinkedIn* has an application for the iPhone and BlackBerry that allows you to manage your profile and connect with other professionals.

18. *Trapster* is an application for the iPhone that alerts you to upcoming speed traps when you're driving. This is especially useful when traveling for business in unfamiliar areas.

19. *Skype* has an application for the iPhone and BlackBerry that allows you to place free international calls to anyone in the world.

20. *Paypal* has an application for the iPhone and BlackBerry that allows you to manage your Paypal account. You can check your balance, send invoices, and more.

BUSINESS PUBLICATIONS: PRINT AND ONLINE

1. *Black Enterprise* is an excellent resource for black entrepreneurs and business owners, and required reading for any serious entrepreneur. Also subscribe to the Blackenterprise.com website for daily breaking content. For more info, visit www.BlackEnterprise.com.

2. *TargetMarketNews.com* is a great website that provides daily news and information that's key to keeping

abreast of the black consumer market, which spends over $1 trillion annually.

3. *The Wall Street Journal* is not just for investors. It's a great daily read. It features lots of news that's relevant to small businesses. If you don't want to pay for the annual subscription, you should at least visit its website daily at www.WSJ.com.

4. *Savoy Professional* is a good resource for black entrepreneurs and corporate executives looking for tools and resources to help grow your business and career. For more details, visit www.savoypro100.com.

5. *Revenue* reports on performance-based marketing and is an excellent resource for all internet marketers. For more info, visit www.RevenueToday.com.

6. *BusinessWeek.com* reports on business news for both major corporations and small businesses. The news articles are often intriguing, and it often publishes columns and editorials with very helpful tips.

7. *DiversityInc.com* is a great online resource for the latest news about diversity and corporate America.

8. *Monarch* caters to the African American professional elite and profiles local business leaders. For more info, visit www.MonarchMagazine.com.

9. *ShePreneur* is an online business magazine concentrating on leadership, development, and life balance for African American women. For more details, visit www.Shepreneur.com.

10. *MarketingProfs.com* publishes daily content about the latest marketing strategies, marketing ideas, and case studies.

11. *DMnews.com* is a good resource for the latest news and information pertaining to direct, database, and online marketing and advertising.

12. *PRweek.com* offers the latest news and commentary pertaining to the public relations industry.

13. *AdAge.com* is the number one resource for the global advertising industry.

14. Read *MBE* (Minority Business Entrepreneur) magazine, a bi-monthly publication and nationwide forum for minority and women business owners. For more details, visit www.MBEmag.com.

15. *Inc.* is a daily resource for entrepreneurs. It's not my favorite, but it's worth glancing at from time to time. For more details, visit www.Inc.com.

16. *Forbes* and Forbes.com offer international business news and commentary.

17. *Fast Company* and FastCompany.com empower business innovators and highlight creative individuals who are sparking change in the marketplace.

18. *Entrepreneur* and Entrepreneur.com focus mostly on small business news, tips, and resources. This is probably my favorite non-black business publication.

19. *Wired* and Wired.com lead the industry in reporting on the latest developments in technology, gadgets, Internet applications, and key players who will impact your business.

20. *African Business* offers cutting edge reporting about the world of business in Africa. This is a great periodical if you're interested in going international. For more details, visit www.africasia.com/africanbusiness.

21. BizJournals.com offers daily business news relevant to various cities, such as Atlanta, Dallas, Los Angeles, and many others.

22. *Website Magazine* provides useful expert information to website professionals. For more info, visit www.websitemagazine.com.

TOP BUSINESS BLOGS

1. DanteLee.com offers daily free tips, ideas, and strategies designed for African American small business owners.

2. Donald Trump gives away great business advice on his blog at www.TrumpUniversity.com/blog.

3. BlackWeb20.com reports on the latest happenings in the world of the black internet.

4. TechCrunch.com is a blog that reports on the latest technology and internet developments.

5. Freakonomics.com, based on the best-selling book by Stephen Dubner, is a blog about "the hidden side of everything" in economics.

6. SocialWayne.com is a blog by technologist Wayne Sutton about the world of social networking.

7. IanFernando.com is a daily blog by internet marketing guru Ian Fernando. He publishes daily tips and news pertaining to affiliate marketing.

8. TopRankBlog.com has some really good daily advice and insight on digital PR, social networking, and search-engine marketing.

9. Mashable.com is the world's largest blog focused exclusively on Web 2.0 and social media news.

10. The Official Google Blog gives you first-hand insight into the products and technology of the most popular internet company in the world. For more info, visit http://googleblog.blogspot.com.

11. ShoeMoney.com is a daily blog with tips and insight pertaining to making money online.

12. BlogMaverick.com is the blog of Mark Cuban, internet billionaire and owner of the Dallas Mavericks.

13. Consumerist.com is a blog that empowers consumers by informing and entertaining them about the top consumer issues of the day.

14. PersonalBrandingBlog.com offers daily tips on how to enhance your personal brand.

15. InventHelp's blog is a great resource for inventors looking to launch their invention ideas. For more info, visit http://blog.inventhelp.com.

16. ThinkingHomeBusiness.com offers daily advice on blogging, podcasting, and social networking for home-based professionals and entrepreneurs.

17. AffiliateTip.com is a blog by affiliate marketer Shawn Collins that reports on the latest developments in the world of affiliate marketing.

18. SEOmoz.org is a blog for search marketers worldwide, providing education, tools, resources, and paid services to help every SEO be the best it can be.

19. BloggingWhileBrown.com promotes intellectual, social, and cultural development of the blogging community by bringing bloggers of color together in one location.

TOP WEBSITES

1. Blackenterprise.com—*Black Enterprise* magazine's website.

2. Blackbusinesslist.com—a black business search-engine.

3. Smallbusinessnotes.com—provides information and resources for small business owners.

4. TheRoot.com—*The Root* is a daily online magazine that provides thought-provoking commentary on today's news from a variety of black perspectives.

5. Startupjournal.com—*The Wall Street Journal*'s Center for Entrepreneurs.

6. Utexas.edu/research/centerblackbusiness—The University of Texas at Austin's Center for Black Business History, Entrepreneurship, and Technology.

7. Izania.com—a black online networking community.

8. Zeromillion.com—an entrepreneurial online resource site.

9. Frasernet.com—a network for black professionals worldwide.

10. Blackpr.com—an extensive African American newswire service.

11. Blackamericaweb.com—Tom Joyner's website for Black America.

12. Blacknews.com—an online portal for black news.

13. Tavistalks.com—Tavis Smiley's website.

14. Blackvoices.com—AOL's website for African Americans.

15. Bet.com—Black Entertainment Television's website.

16. Thegriot.com—a video-centric news community devoted to covering stories and perspectives that affect and reflect the African American community.

17. Entrepreneur.com—an online and print small business publication. Information to help start, grow, or manage a small business.

18. Inc.com—a website focused on business resources for the entrepreneur.

19. Forbes.com—a source for the latest business and financial news and analysis, covering personal finance, lifestyle, technology, and stock markets.

20. Readwriteweb.com—a popular weblog that provides web technology news, reviews, and analysis, covering web apps, web technology trends, and social networking.

PROFESSIONAL DEVELOPMENT

1. The Black Enterprise Entrepreneurs Conference and Expo is probably my favorite. In the past, it's been held in Detroit, Orlando, and Dallas, among other cities. It's probably the biggest black business conference of the year, and well worth attending. For more info, visit www.BlackEnterprise.com/events/entrepreneurs-conference.

2. The FraserNet PowerNetworking conference is usually held in Atlanta, and it's a great place to meet other African American entrepreneurs. For more info, follow it on Twitter @FraserNet or visit www.FraserNet.com.

3. The Black Enterprise Women of Power Summit is probably the biggest conference for black women

entrepreneurs and professionals. For more info, visit www.BlackEnterprise.com/WPS.

4. Affiliate Summit is a great series of conferences that focus on the industry of affiliate marketing. Affiliate marketing is performance-based marketing, and many make anywhere from thousands to millions a year doing it. The conferences are usually held in Las Vegas, New York, and Miami. For more details, visit www.AffiliateSummit.com.

5. Affiliate Convention is another event for the affiliate marketing industry. It's free for affiliates to attend, and the seminars are very informative. For more details, visit www.AffiliateConvention.com.

6. Ad Tech is an international series of conferences that focus on interactive advertising and technology dedicated to connecting all sides of today's brand marketing landscape. For more details, visit www.Ad-Tech.com.

7. The National Association of Market Developers (NAMD) annual conference serves as a national African American consumer resource. The conference is generally held on the east coast or in the Midwest. For more info, visit www.namdintl.org.

8. The National Black Public Relations Society (NBPRS) Conference is a gathering for African Americans in the public relations industry. For more info, visit www.nbprs.org.

9. The Blogging While Brown annual conference is a great event to learn about the latest blogging strategies and techniques. It's the only event that's exclusively for African American bloggers. For more details, follow it on Twitter @BWBconference or visit www.BloggingWhileBrown.com.

10. The Black Millionaire's Summit was founded by Russell Simmons and WNBA Champion Fran Harris. For more details, visit www.BlackMillionairesSummit.com.

11. The National Sales Network annual conference is designed to assist African American sales professionals across all industries in developing the skills required to ensure that they're competitive in the fast-paced, ever-changing sales environment. For more details, visit www.SalesNetwork.org.

12. African American Empowerment Weekend is a conference designed to empower black professionals and entrepreneurs. For more details, visit www.AAEW.org.

13. Black World and New Media Expo is the first and only industry-wide conference, trade show, and media event for all new media. For more details, visit www. blogworldexpo.com.

14. Search Marketing Expo is the largest series of expos that focus entirely on organic and PPC search-engine marketing. For more details, visit www. SearchMarketingExpo.com.

15. PubCon is an educational conference and industry trade show programmed specifically for web professionals and website owners. For more info, visit www.PubCon.com.

16. The African American Internet Summit and the MAAX Summit (Marketing to African Americans with eXcellence), are two conferences hosted by industry veteran Ken Smikle and his company, Target Market News. These are events relevant for black website owners and marketers. For more details, visit www. targetmarketnews.com.

17. The African American Business Summit/Turning Point Urban Business Expo delivers resources, information, and empowerment to the small businesses that are the growth engine for America's economy. For more info visit www.tpurbiz.com.

18. The ANA Multicultural Marketing Conference goes well beyond the basics to delve into the current role of multicultural marketing and where it may be headed in the future. For more info, visit www.ana.net/events/content/anaevents.

19. The Black Consumer Research and Advertising Summit is the only industry conference devoted exclusively to African American marketing, media, and consumer research. For more details, visit www.targetmarketnews.com.

20. StrategyandPerformance.com offers a complimentary executive coaching assessment and audio download, plus free access to articles on strategy and organizational performance.

21. Chris Musselwhite's Discovery Learning (www.discoverylearning.com) website offers case studies, articles, research summaries, and newsletters on training and leadership—all for free.

22. Roger Pearman's website (www.qualifying.org) and bookstore (www.qualifying.org/bookstore) provide industry leading training and certification in MBTI®, Strong Interest Indicator®, emotional intelligence assessment, leadership coaching, and other personal and organizational development tools.

23. CEOExpress.com (http://www.ceoexpress.com/default.asp) is a one-stop source for links to hundreds of resources on business news, business research, office tools, and leisure for busy executives.

24. The Center for Creative Leadership (http://www.ccl.
org/CCLCommerce/index.aspx) is an internationally
recognized resource for leadership development
for individuals and organizations. Of particular
interest on its website are the more than 250 pages of
leadership articles and resources you can access for
free, including excerpts of reports and presentations,
as well as full articles.

25. The Aji Network (http://www.ajinet.com/excerpts_
papers.html). Inc.com columnist and founder and
CEO of The Aji Network, Toby Hecht, offers excerpts
from his popular program that shows business
owners and executives how to fulfill their ambitions
in business and in life. The website, while offering
an overview of Hecht's educational philosophy and
programs, offers links to excerpts from assignments
and papers written for his programs.

26. The Tom Peters Company website TomPeters.com
(http://www.tompeters.com/index.php) has its own
blog and lists many more that touch on leadership
and management. It also offers links to interviews
with what the web staff at the site call "Cool Friends,"
including Richard Florida, Dan Pink, Paco Underhill,
and other notable book authors.

ENTREPRENEUR AND SMALL BUSINESS COMPETITIONS

1. UPS Best Out-of-the-Box Small Business Contest. This
national contest honors the most innovative small
businesses in the U.S. Prize: $10,000 cash or $10,000
in free UPS shipping (www.ups.com/outofthebox).

2. The World of Difference Awards Contest. An
opportunity for your small business to discover the
potential of technology. Prize: $100,000 in hardware,
software, and services (www.theworldofdifference.org).

3. Dell/NFIB Small Business Excellence Award. A contest sponsored by Dell Computer and the National Federation of Independent Business. Prize: $30,000 in tech gear and services (www.dell.com/ceaward).

4. The Miller Urban Entrepreneurs Series. Offers adults 21 to 35 an opportunity to enter its Business Plan Competition. Prize: $50,000, $20,000, or $2,500 in grants (http://www.millerbrewing.com/inthecommunity/urban).

5. The Make Mine a Million $ Business Award (www.makemineamillion.org). It provides a combination of coaching, financing, and marketing tools that women entrepreneurs need to help grow their businesses from micro to millions. Eligible businesses are at least 50 percent owned by at least one woman who is a U.S. citizen or legal resident, have been in business at least two years, and have annual revenues of at least $200,000.

TRADE SHOWS TIPS

1. If your company can provide a service that will benefit the trade show, offer to do so in exchange for a free booth. Many event holders will accept your offer.

2. When staffing a booth, don't just sit there and let potential customers walk by. Stand up and engage people as they pass. Have materials in your hand to give to those who may not have time to stop and talk.

3. Don't overcrowd your table. Just because there's space available doesn't mean that you have to fill it with needless or surplus material. Keep it simple and organized.

4. Collect business cards. Your booth should always have a clear container in which people may leave their cards. Even if you have to step away, people will know to leave their cards. This will help you easily follow up with people later.

5. Make sure your signage is professional, colorful, and clean cut. FedEx Office has a very affordable service for printing big signs and posters.

6. Give away bags with your logo and company name on it. Many times, people at trade shows will gladly take an extra bag because they've accumulated so much material. When they're carrying around your bag, that's free advertising.

7. Give away prizes, such as T-shirts, duffle bags, or baseball caps with your company's logo.

8. No matter how tired you are, attend a few seminars and all the group meals. Target industry leaders and contacts you want to meet. Spend some time each day circulating and schmoozing.

9. When you finally catch up with a person you want to meet, ask them to join you outside the hall where it's quieter. If it's an industry leader, you'll only have a few minutes to make an impression before they're distracted or led away.

10. Speak to as many people as you can while waiting in buffet or bathroom lines. You never know who will turn out to be a great contact.

11. If a reporter or producer approaches you, give a good quote for their story.

12. Rather than carrying around heavy brochures, collect the cards of serious prospects. Say, "So many people were interested in my products, I've already given all

my brochures away. But, I'd love to send you one as soon as I get back to the office."

13. Distribute postcards. Unlike a heavy brochure, postcards are light and easy to carry. They are also very inexpensive to print. For about $500, you can get 5,000 postcards made by 1-800-POSTCARDS.

14. Bring three times as many business cards as you think you'll need.

15. Wear comfortable clothes and a jacket with pockets. Park your personal business cards for hand-out in one pocket and store cards that you receive in another.

16. If you don't have a stylish, comfortable outfit to make a good impression, go shopping before the show.

17. Give yourself extra time—you'll need it. Don't take the last flight out the evening before you're supposed to be at the trade show. You'll be cutting it too close if there's a delay. Among the most common are flight-delaying thunderstorms, which tend to occur in the afternoon.

18. Be aware of expensive cab fares. Getting from airport to convention center presents wrinkles. In many cities the convention center is close to the airport, which means a taxi can be an affordable alternative to taking the shuttle bus. Especially if there is no bus. If you're visiting a city for the first time, find the information desk and ask for the names and business cards of reputable cab companies, and get an estimate of price and drive time to your hotel.

19. Orient yourself to new surroundings early. Find out how far the hotel is from the convention center. Get a map of the neighborhood. But remember, if the map shows your hotel is five blocks away, five blocks in Manhattan is not the same as five blocks in Peoria.

LOCAL BUSINESS TIPS

1. If you have a local business, you should get listed on Local.com—a very popular search-engine that people use when looking for local services and products.

2. Local businesses can get a free listing on YellowPages.com. They also have an affordable service where you can pay to advertise using a pay-per-click model. For more details, visit http://listings.yellowpages.com.

3. SuperPages.com offers a pay-per-click advertising service for local businesses. For more details, visit http://advertising.superpages.com.

4. Always subscribe to your local black newspaper. The cost is generally no more than $20 a year. This will help you to be aware of the black business developments in your area.

5. If you have a local business, consider hanging promotional door hangers on people's doors. 48HourPrint.com can help you with this for a very reasonable price.

6. Make sure you're listed in your local "Who's Who in Black . . ." directory. It's free and will make it easier for local business leaders to find you. For more details, visit www.whoswhopublishing.com.

7. Consider advertising on LocalAdLink.com, an online directory of local businesses.

8. If your business is in an area where people have to pay to park, always validate parking. Many people will come into your storefront and buy something just to get free parking.

9. When people come into your storefront (whether they buy or not), always get their e-mail addresses. Before

you know it, you'll have hundreds or even thousands of them to e-mail people regarding your new products and upcoming specials.

10. Consider advertising on local radio stations. Contrary to local belief, this is very affordable. Often the station will create your commercial for you, for free.

11. Consider advertising on local television stations. Pricing can be as low as $30 to have your commercial viewed by thousands of people in your local area. The cost to get a commercial created can be as low as $300.

12. Consider register tape advertising—advertising on the back of grocery store receipts. Not all, but many grocery stores, such as Krogers and Ralphs, allow you to do this. It's very affordable and very effective.

NETWORKING TIPS

1. Stop being a business card distributor—passing out business cards like flyers. Not only are you wasting your time, but you're also wasting your cards. Focus more on getting others' business cards so that you can follow up with them later. Don't depend on people to follow up with you.

2. Be genuine and authentic. When networking, don't pretend you're someone you're not. Be yourself and act normal.

3. Follow through quickly. Shaking a hand and getting a business card is just the first step. Be sure to follow up promptly via e-mail or phone.

4. Be patient. If you're following up with someone you recently met, be patient if they don't respond right away. Many people are very busy, and are not fast

responders. You don't want to leave multiple voice messages and send multiple e-mails. That can be a deterrent.

5.   Be quick about describing what you do. When networking with others, you should be able to describe what you do very easily and swiftly. If it takes too long, you'll lose people's attention.

6.   Ask open-ended questions. In other words, ask questions that require more than just a "yes" or "no" answer. This will impress people and show them you're genuinely interested in what they do.

7.   If you want to network more often than you are now, consider holding a volunteer position in a local or national organization. This will keep you visible and constantly in a room full of people.

8.   Another way to network more is to attend local business chamber meetings. Usually, these are held at least once a month—and people are free to attend.

KEY ORGANIZATIONS

1.   Register as a minority supplier with the National Minority Supplier Development Council (NMSDC). Doing so will give you the proper certification to do business with government agencies and major corporations. For more details, visit www.nmsdc.org.

2.   Join the National Association for the Self-Employed (NASE). It is a leading resource for self-employed people, and offers a lot of group discounts on health insurance and more. For more info, visit www.NASE.org.

3.   The National Association of Women Business Owners (NAWBO) is the unified voice of America's more than

10 million women-owned businesses, representing the fastest growing segment of the market. For more info, visit www.NAWBO.org.

4.   The National Minority Business Council, Inc. (NMBC) has been helping small, minority-, and women-owned businesses succeed for over a quarter century. For more details, visit www.nmbc.org.

5.   Black Business Builders Club is a membership organization of positive, progressive, and proactive entrepreneurs, business owners, internet marketers, consumers, and students. For more details, visit www. BlackBusinessBuildersClub.com.

6.   The National Black MBA Association (NBMBAA) is the most powerful social network of individuals dedicated to increasing corporate diversity and access to capital. For more information, visit www.nbmbaa.org.

7.   The National Black Business Council is a nonprofit organization dedicated to the creation and advancement of African American and minority-owned businesses. For more details, visit www.nbbc.org.

8.   The United States Association for Small Business and Entrepreneurship (USASBE) is the leading voice in entrepreneurship research, teaching, and application. For more details, visit www.usasbe.org.

9.   Business and Professional Women/USA (BPW/USA) is an organization that provides women professionals with access to local meeting and networking opportunities. For more details, visit www.bpwusa.org.

TOP CONFERENCES FOR BLACK ENTREPRENEURS

1. Ad Tech. An interactive advertising and technology conference dedicated to connecting all sides of today's brand marketing landscape. For more info, visit www. ad-tech.com.

2. Affiliate Summit. This conference addresses the latest developments and news in the affiliate marketing industry. Any company with a high-traffic website should attend. For more info, visit www. affiliatesummit.com/08w_conference.php.

3. Black Enterprise Entrepreneurs Conference. Features four days of business, motivational, and leadership seminars designed to empower and profit emerging and established minority businesses. For more info, visit www.blackenterprise.com/events/beec.asp.

4. Black Enterprise Women of Power Summit. This four-day career enhancement conference creates an environment that promotes cooperation and encourages attendees to network, bond, share strategies, and learn from each other's experience. For more info, visit www.blackenterprise.com/events/wps/ wps.asp

5. FraserNet Conference. Founded by George Fraser, this conference encourages a global leadership network committed to economic development through education, training, and empowerment for black people. For more info, visit www.frasernet.com.

6. NAMD Conference. This conference, sponsored by the National Association of Market Developers, communicates resources of consumer information, industry skill, and expertise in the African-American consumer market. For more info, visit www.namdntl. org/conference.htm.

7. NBPRS National Conference. This national conference, hosted by the National Society of Black Public Relations, is a great resource for those in the PR industry. It's also a great event for those looking to better understand public relations. For more info, visit www.nbprs.org.

8. Blogging While Brown Conference (www. bloggingwhilebrown.com). Created as a way to give bloggers of color—dissatisfied with the amount of diversity in some of the larger blogging conferences— an opportunity to discuss current issues and to learn about the latest technology that will assist them in disseminating their work.

9. African American Internet Summit (www. targetmarketnews.com). Sponsored by Target Market News this conference is the nation's only conference devoted to the latest trends and opportunities in targeting the $800 billion Black consumer market through online and mobile media.

FREE STUFF

1. FreeTradeMagazines.com and FreeBizMag.com offer 100 percent free subscriptions to hundreds of different business magazines.

2. Score.org offers a free and confidential small business mentoring service.

3. Vistaprint.com offers free business cards, but you have to pay for shipping and other upgrade options.

4. Donald Trump's TrumpUniversity.com offers free consultations and a free introductory course on real estate investing.

5. ToolKit.com offers a free small business toolkit with access to free webinars, a free business guide, and a free newsletter.

6. TechSoup.org offers free and discounted software to companies that are also non-profit organizations. You can choose from over 340 different products from companies such as Microsoft, Adobe, and Symantec.

7. 1FreeCart.com offers free online shopping cart software. You can set up your very own online store that accepts credit cards for free—with no monthly hosting fees.

8. FreeBooksForAll.com is devoted to giving away free downloadable books on business, economics, personal finance, and computers.

9. GoReadGreen.com gives away free one-year digital subscriptions to any magazine of your choice.

10. FreeConferenceCall.com allows you to do free telephone conferencing with up to 97 people simultaneously.

11. Xpenser.com is a free business expense tracking tool that allows you to record expenses from any device— e-mail, SMS, voice (call and say your expense), IM, Twitter, iPhone, or BlackBerry.

12. PostcardMania gives away free postcard samples and an information pack to give you some fresh ideas. For more details, visit www.postcardmania.com/free-samples.

13. Stock.Xchng is the largest free stock photography site on the internet with a library of over 350,000 free-use photographs. The high-resolution photographs are professionally done and can be used free of charge on

your website, presentation, or business card. For more details, visit www.sxc.hu.

14. 000WebHost.com offers top-class free web hosting services without advertising! There are no hidden costs, no advertisements, and no restrictive terms.

15. Inc.com has a library of sample forms, job description templates, interactive worksheets, spreadsheets, and contracts, such as: Work for Hire Agreement, Articles of Incorporation Form, Articles of Incorporation Template, How to Set Business Goals, How to Determine Your Own Salary, How to Make the Most of Customer Feedback, and many more.

ACKNOWLEDGMENTS

Writing "Black Business Secrets" was a multi-phase project that took nearly two years to complete, and I'm very appreciative of all who helped me along the way. I must first credit Denise Pines of The Smiley Group, who introduced my work to Tavis Smiley. And of course, I thank Tavis Smiley for recognizing the book's potential and deciding to publish it.

In the past, I've done business with Mr. Smiley, have been featured on his radio show, and have addressed his Youth Leadership Institute as a speaker. To now be a member of his publishing family, SmileyBooks, is a great honor.

Next, I would like to thank Cheryl Woodruff, president and associate publisher of SmileyBooks, for her guidance, expertise, and extensive assistance in editing the book and bringing it to life. Thanks also to the SmileyBooks team including Kira Citron, for doing for me what I do for others in the PR and marketing of my book, and Kirsten Melvey for her invaluable efforts.

No book is complete without a really organized and educated researcher, and Pittershawn Palmer of Creative Ankh was just that. I'm thankful for her extensive research, insight, and commentary that she contributed. I'd also like to thank my former intern, Brian Sherman, for helping with proofreading and editing; and my receptionist, Charlene Mikaelian, for on-going support and dedicated management of our superstar entrepreneur interviews.

Special thanks to Will Moss, for being a supportive and intellectual business partner and a close friend for the past 10 years; and to Patricia Means for being a great friend and my first business mentor who always encouraged me to pursue my goals. Both have been extremely influential in shaping me into the business person that I have become, and the success that I have achieved.

I must also thank Dr. Randal Pinkett for taking the time to write the foreword for this book, and the following superstar entrepreneurs for generously sharing their wisdom with us: Bob Johnson, George Fraser, Karen Hunter, Tom Burrell, Wally Amos, Dr. Farrah Gray, Stephanie Drake, Ephren Taylor, Nadine Thompson, Gwen Richardson, and C. Sunny Martin. Their insights have been a huge asset to this project.

I'm especially grateful to Irvin and Beverly Lee, for being such amazing and supportive parents and always pushing me forward on the road to success. As far back as I can remember, my parents have always played an active and inspirational role in my life.

I'm truly grateful to have a son, Dante Lee, Jr. (DJ), and I'm thanking him in advance because I know that one day he too will be a successful entrepreneur.

ABOUT THE AUTHOR

Dante Lee is the president and CEO of Diversity City Media, an African American marketing and public relations firm based in Columbus, Ohio. Founded in 2000, this award-winning company, known for its marquee online businesses—BlackPR.com and BlackNews.com—helps its clients, from corporations to start ups, penetrate the African American consumer market.

Showcased in *Ebony's* 2010 Young Entrepreneurs List, Lee is a respected motivational speaker and diversity consultant. He is also the co-founder of social networking powerhouse Lee Moss Media, whose properties attract over two million African American visitors each month.

SmileyBooks Titles of Related Interest

DVD

STAND: a film by Tavis Smiley

BOOKS

AMERICA I AM LEGENDS:
Rare Moments and Inspiring Words
Edited by SmileyBooks; foreword by Tavis Smiley

AMERICA I AM BLACKFACTS:
The Timelines of African American History 1601–2008
by Quintard Taylor

BRAINWASHED:
Challenging the Myth of Black Inferiority, by Tom Burrell

EVERYTHING I'M NOT MADE ME EVERYTHING I AM
Discovering Your Personal Best, by Jeff Johnson

NEVER MIND SUCCESS . . . GO FOR GREATNESS!
The Best Advice I've Ever Received, by Tavis Smiley

CARD DECKS

EMPOWERMENT CARDS: A-50 CARD DECK
by Tavis Smiley

EMPOWERMENT CARDS FOR INSPIRED LIVING
by Tavis Smiley

All of the above are available at your local bookstore, or
may be ordered online through our distributor, Hay House,
(see contact information on last page).

• ▣ • ▣ • ▣ •

We hoped you enjoyed this SMILEYBOOKS publication.
If you would like to receive additional information, please contact:

SMILEYBOOKS

Distributed by:
Hay House, Inc.
P.O. Box 5100
Carlsbad, CA 92018-5100
(760) 431-7695 or **(800) 654-5126**
(760) 431-6948 (fax) or **(800) 650-5115 (fax)**
www.hayhouse.com® • **www.hayfoundation.org**

• ▣ • ▣ • ▣ •

Published and distributed in Australia by: Hay House Australia Pty. Ltd.
18/36 Ralph St. • Alexandria NSW 2015 • Phone: 612-9669-4299
Fax: 612-9669-4144 • www.hayhouse.com.au

Published and distributed in the United Kingdom by:
Hay House UK, Ltd. • 292B Kensal Rd., London W10 5BE • Phone:
44-20-8962-1230 • Fax: 44-20-8962-1239 • www.hayhouse.co.uk

Published and distributed in the Republic of South Africa by:
Hay House SA (Pty), Ltd., P.O. Box 990, Witkoppen 2068 • Phone/Fax:
27-11-467-8904 • info@hayhouse.co.za • www.hayhouse.co.za

Published and Distributed in India by: Hay House Publishers India,
Muskaan Complex, Plot No. 3, B-2, Vasant Kunj, New Delhi 110 070
Phone: 91-11-4176-1620 • Fax: 91-11-4176-1630 • www.hayhouse.co.in

Distributed in Canada by: Raincoast • 9050 Shaughnessy St.,
Vancouver, B.C. V6P 6E5 • Phone: (604) 323-7100 • Fax: (604) 323-2600

• ▣ • ▣ • ▣ •.